11/98

29.95

Till Freedom Cried Out

NUMBER SIX:
*The Clayton Wheat Williams
Texas Life Series*

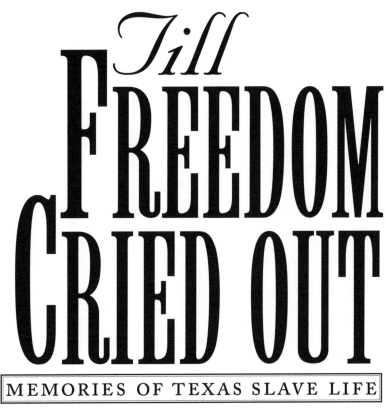

Till FREEDOM CRIED OUT

MEMORIES OF TEXAS SLAVE LIFE

Edited by T. Lindsay Baker and Julie P. Baker

Illustrated by Kermit Oliver

Texas A&M University Press
College Station

Library of Congress Cataloging-in-Publication Data

Till freedom cried out : memories of Texas slave life / edited by T. Lindsay
    Baker and Julie P. Baker.
            p.   cm. — (The Clayton Wheat Williams Texas life series ; no. 6)
    ISBN 0-89096-736-9
    1. Slaves—Texas—Interviews. 2. Slavery—Texas—History—19th
century. 3. Plantation life—Texas—History—19th century. 4. Oral
history. I. Baker, T. Lindsay. II. Baker, Julie P. (Julie Philips), 1943–   .
III. Series.
E444.T55   1997
976.4´00496—dc20   96-38575
                                                                        CIP

Contents

Contents

· · · · · · · · ·

VI

Illustrations

Preface

Cast yourself back in time, over half a century ago, to June 21, 1937. Then, the east side of Oklahoma City, known to "white folks" as Colored Town, was dominated by oil derricks that towered over board-and-batten shacks and other humble structures that housed many of the city's African Americans. Outdoors the nights were illuminated by the flares of natural gas being burned off at the oil wells, and the air, both day and night, smelled of petroleum.

Into this setting came pert Ida Belle Hunter, a black interviewer from the Federal Writers' Project, seeking ninety-five-year-old Harriett Robinson in her home at 524 Lottie Avenue. After a pleasant chat, Hunter began asking Robinson about her life as a slave in Texas. What followed were stories about times long past, tales about events that were nearly unbelievable. Robinson told about slavery days. One incident in particular was about the time Robinson's white master in Texas entered the Confederate Army. While he was gone, Robinson's mistress would beat her slaves unmercifully: "She say, 'You master's out fighting and losing blood trying to save you from them Yankees, so you kin git your'n here.' Miss Julia would take me by the ears and butt my head against the wall." Ida Belle Hunter jotted down the words as quickly as she could while Harriett Robinson narrated her life story. As the steel derricks stood sentinel over the Oklahoma City east side, Robinson and Hunter traveled back in time to Texas ninety years before, to more cruel and bitter days. As the old lady said, "Them was . . . dog days. . . . Meanest woman I ever seen in my whole life."

Ida Belle Hunter and Harriett Robinson were two of many others who played a part in a massive oral history project which took place between 1937 and 1939. As part of the Works Progress Administration, the Federal Writers' Project had been established to put unemployed people into paying jobs during the Great Depression. The project hired white-collar workers to undertake specific writing projects, many of them related to state and local history. In addition to the responsibility of producing a series of city and state guidebooks, the interviewers were also charged with seeking out aged Americans to ask them about their life experiences. In Texas they talked to old ranchers and oil field workers, and on the Atlantic coast they recorded the memories of seamen and shipmasters. In seventeen states with sufficient black population to support the project, field interviewers recorded the memories of elderly African Americans who had lived during slavery days. In Oklahoma about a quarter of the one hundred thirty ex-slave interviews came from men and women who had been slaves in Texas but who had later moved to Oklahoma. Because these interviews had been intermixed with those of other ex-slaves in the Sooner State, they were long overlooked by Texas historians, who instead have used stories from former bondmen interviewed in Texas. Typescripts of those narratives are housed in one version at the Center for American History at the University of Texas at Austin and in a somewhat different form at the Library of Congress and are the product of the W.P.A. Texas Slave Narrative Project. The purpose of this book is to bring home from across the Red River the remembrances of Texas' ex-slaves.

The Federal Writers' Project had its beginning in summer, 1935. That fall individual writers' projects were initiated in each of the forty-eight states, and unemployed writers, with varied backgrounds, were hired to start work on state guidebooks. But from the earliest days of the state projects, as part of the research for the state guides, field reporters interviewed aged residents. As reports arrived in the Washington, D.C., headquarters, administration officials soon recognized the value of this information for black history. After some consideration, administrators launched a separate program designed specifically to locate and interview elderly blacks about their experiences in slavery. Although it remained subordinate to the broader goal of preparing state guidebooks, the Slave Narrative Project got underway in seventeen southern and border states. In the spring of 1937, field interviewers from South Carolina to Oklahoma officially began searching for and interviewing these ex-slaves.

The Oklahoma Federal Writers' Project began operations in November, 1935, under project director William Cunningham. A year and a half later, field interviewers began work on the Oklahoma Slave Narrative Project. Although administrative records remaining from the Oklahoma project are sketchy, they shed some light on how the interviews were conducted.

Field interviewers employed a set of standardized questions that had been developed by John A. Lomax, national director of folklore for the Federal Writers' Project. His list of suggested questions helped the reporters seek more substantive information from the interviewees and provided uniformity to the format of the narratives. In addition to these questions, interviewers were free to ask the respondents a variety of further questions—about foodways, social history (church affiliation, how they had learned about the slaves' being freed), and health, medical, and folk practices. Although the questions were edited out of the narratives, this format of standard inquiries was also intended to make it easy to compare the informants' responses on these frequently repeated topics.

After each interview, field personnel submitted field notes to editorial writers in the office, who then revised and typed then into various intermediate drafts. The final copy was prepared according to the project's style and format guidelines, with interviewers' questions omitted. On completion of the final draft, project personnel then forwarded an original copy and a carbon copy of each interview to a central clearinghouse in Washington, D.C.

Work on the narratives progressed through the remainder of 1937 and into early 1938, until the attention of most state and national project administrators was diverted by new projects and the approaching deadlines for the production of the state guidebooks. Although interviews of former slaves decreased dramatically in 1938, a few additional narratives were compiled through that year, until the Writers' Project ended in 1939.

At the close of the Federal Writers' Project, approximately twenty-three hundred typewritten slave narratives were transferred to the Writers' Unit at the Library of Congress. There they lay dormant for a number of months until Benjamin A. Botkin, who had succeeded John A. Lomax, began organizing the transcripts for permanent archival preservation. The original typescript copies, now bound in large grayish green volumes, were eventually housed in the Manuscript Division of the Library of Congress, along with various supplementary materials and carbon copies, which were filed separately.

In more ways than they realized, the interviewers had a profound effect on the narratives. Limited information is available on the personnel who participated in the Oklahoma Slave Narrative Project. However, records indicate that at the height of the project field interviewers included three African Americans (Willie Allen, Ida Belle Hunter, and Bertha P. Tipton), one Native American (Ethel Wolfe Garrison), and six whites (Jessie R. Ervin, Robert Vinson Lackey, L. P. Livingston, J. S. Thomas, Craig Vollmer, and Lura J. Wilson). Unlike many other states, where only whites found employment in the project, Oklahoma reflected greater ethnic diversity in its staff, which may have contributed to the candidness of the interviews.

And that candidness may have also been the result of the interviewer's own sense of conscientiousness and responsibility. In the fall of 1937 Jessie

R. Ervin wrote to project state headquarters, explaining the concerns she had about the quality of her work: "I could have made it [the interview] longer perhaps, if I had been sure it was acceptable. . . . My interviews are short but I find them such a repetition that I do not write all they tell me." She continued, describing herself as a "rank amateur" at the typewriter, "It is real labor for me and I am ashamed of every article that I send but . . . I have been sending them on." Ervin need not have worried, for her interviews are among the finest of the Oklahoma ex-slave narratives.

In fact, the Oklahoma interviews from the Federal Writers' Project played an important role in the Slave Narrative Project because of their superior quality. Although the seventy-five Oklahoma interviews sent to Washington represent less than half of 1 percent of all the narratives now in the Library of Congress collection, the Oklahoma interviews are considered among the best and have served as a major source for scholarly research about slavery. In 1945, during the assembly of materials for his book based on the W.P.A. slave narratives, Botkin himself selected from the Oklahoma interviews over 11 percent of the narratives and extracts that appear in his book *Lay My Burden Down*. In 1970 author Norman R. Yetman also recognized the superiority of the Oklahoma, North Carolina, and Texas narratives and included them in his book, *Voices from Slavery: Selections from the Slave Narratives Collection of the Library of Congress*. Fifteen percent of the interview transcripts he identified as "the finest" in the entire Library of Congress collection came from Oklahoma informants. And in 1988, 10 percent of the narratives that James Mellon used in full in *Bullwhip Days: The Slaves Remember* came from Oklahoma interviews; over 4 percent of the brief extracts in the book also came from Oklahoma sources.

But not all the Oklahoma slave narratives made their way to Washington. Fifty-five ex-slave interviews, which were never forwarded by Oklahoma Federal Writers' Project personnel, are preserved only in Oklahoma City at the Oklahoma Historical Society, as typed or handwritten manuscripts, exactly as the W.P.A. workers prepared them in the 1930s. They remain there to this day.

Until 1972 the W.P.A. slave narratives in the Library of Congress and in Oklahoma City were available only in their original typewritten form. That year historian George P. Rawick began a multiyear project to locate and publish W.P.A. slave narratives not only in the Library of Congress but in repositories throughout the Unites States as well. The result of his search was the forty-one–volume *The American Slave: A Composite Autobiography*, which includes all the interviews in this book, except those by Eliza Elsey, Sonny Greer, and Alice Rawlings. Since Rawick's edition usually can be found only in academic libraries, few general readers have had access to the materials, until 1996, when *The W.P.A. Oklahoma Slave Narratives* was published by the University of Oklahoma Press in a comprehensive single-volume annotated edition. It includes all the known W.P.A. Oklahoma slave narratives.

Just as the interviewers affected the quality of the narratives, the guidelines provided by the national headquarters of the Federal Writers' Project shaped the text. To ensure literary consistency in the finished drafts, each state office was furnished with specific guidance for transcribing African American speech and dialect. But in reality editors in Oklahoma produced interview transcripts with varying dialectical representations, and field workers were encouraged to record idioms precisely.

The slave narrative texts from Oklahoma are a rich and diverse source of information. The interviews usually consist of a first or subsequent draft and a final edited draft on standard 8½ by 11-inch typing paper, required by the Washington office. Whereas the Library of Congress narratives consist only of final drafts, along with separately filed carbon copies, content appraisal sheets, and supplementary materials, the narratives preserved in the Archives and Manuscripts Division of the Oklahoma Historical Society include more background information. There most of the interviews can be found in file folders which may also contain handwritten field notes, handwritten or typewritten preliminary drafts, later typewritten drafts, and final typewritten drafts, all generally on 8½ by 11-inch typing paper of varying quality, some of it yellowed and brittle. But there can also be found some notes and office memoranda related to the interviews. And a few fuzzy carbon copies of final drafts sent to Washington have also survived. Important insights into the editing process are preserved in the Oklahoma Historical Society materials, for many of the first and subsequent drafts bear the editors' handwritten notations for changes marked in either ink or pencil, which document how the actual interview material was modified to fit the way clerical staff interpreted national project standards. Additionally, both the Library of Congress and the Oklahoma Historical Society collections contain interviews not preserved in the other's holdings.

Like most historical evidence, the slave narratives present certain shortcomings. They are filled with contrasts and contradictions, truth and seeming fabrications, paradox and evasions, reflection and exaggeration, but all this variety constitutes the very bread on which historians feed as they seek the truth. Because the narratives come from oral sources, readers today must interpret them with care and healthy skepticism. For this reason, the slave narratives deserve some comments for readers.

The ages of the interviewees present special considerations for modern users of these remembrances. More than two-thirds of the respondents were at least eighty years old when they were interviewed, so age may have dimmed some of their memories. Despite this circumstance, the events they discussed occurred early in their lives and dealt with life-shaping events, such as relocation or separation from family members. Therefore, they are the types of occurrences which people might be expected to remember more clearly. Furthermore, the tradition of storytelling was strong in many African American families, which may have allowed elderly blacks to keep their memories alive by retelling them over the years.

Age also affects the narratives in another way. Because the interviews were recorded in the 1930s, most of the ex-slaves remembered bondage only as children in the 1850s and 1860s. Because the individuals interviewed were young during slavery, they would have generally avoided some of the harsher aspects of discipline exerted on the adults, thus giving them a possibly skewed impression of life in servitude.

Racial attitudes which shaped American life during the 1930s may have also influenced respondents' comments. At a time when Jim Crow laws and white supremacy attitudes prevailed almost unchallenged in the United States and when segregation operated at its most blatant levels, perhaps the race, demeanor, and actions of the field interviewers influenced the content of the interviews and in some instances may have led to distortions and limitations on what the respondents actually said. This book's commentary section, which follows the interviews, provides helpful background information on both the interviewer's race and respondent's age so that the reader can reach an independent conclusion about how these factors may have influenced the interview.

Attention paid to detail, consistency, nuance, and forms of address in the interview may reveal special insights. Evidence of intimacy between interviewer and interviewee may suggest greater levels of candor than in narratives in which formal social distance seems apparent. Positive comments in the text, like "Old Master was always good to us," compared to descriptions of physical or emotional abuse help to illuminate our understanding of the former slave's perspective.

Interviews in this book are arranged in alphabetical order by interviewee's surname. Two narratives each are provided from two of the informants, Lewis Bonner and Lizzie Farmer, from separate interviews in the Library of Congress and the Oklahoma Historical Society. To provide the greatest literary consistency in this volume, the final or most recent draft of each interview is presented exactly as it was prepared by W.P.A. personnel. The commentary section also provides information on the location of all known drafts for the interviews, so readers can secure copies of the earlier versions should they be needed for further study or analysis.

Background information on places, individuals, and incidents mentioned in the interviews can be found in the commentary section. It sometimes corroborates data in the narratives and sometimes disagrees with it. In some instances interviewees did not state where in Texas they were slaves, making it difficult or impossible to locate documentation about their owners, other family members, or related events. Therefore, in those instances, commentary information is not included.

The narratives in this book help us to understand Texas slavery days—a time of interdependence, when black and white lived in greater intimacy but with greater barriers than we know today. The middle years of the nineteenth century, when most of the interviewees were growing to maturity, were years of a preindustrial South in which people lived in the country in daily contact with the land and where family and kin provided essential emotional support. By the 1930s, though, much of their familiar world had ceased to exist. Many of the aged interviewees, living in cities during the depths of the economic depression, were lonely, poor, and sometimes hungry and looked back to a time of shared work, joys, and sorrows. Some even wondered aloud to their interviewers if they might have been better off in servitude.

Although we can learn about slavery from both white and black sources, it is the literate slaveholder class whose records have been produced in remarkable volume. The narratives here provide insights that are lacking from records left by white people, for they are the memories of the slaves themselves. Through their words we hear their personal stories of how it felt to be chattel. Those who read these pages should come and bring their buckets to the well and drink deep of the memories.

Acknowledgments

Many individuals contributed to the publication of these interviews with Texas' former slaves living in Oklahoma during the 1930s. First credits go to the interviewees themselves, who in old age and often in poverty shared their remembrances of former days south of the Red River. And without the efforts and sensitivity of the interviewers, writers, and editors of those narratives, these valuable traces of Texas' African American history would not have survived.

Thanks go to the staff of the Manuscript Division of the Library of Congress for assistance with the narrative final drafts, carbon copies, appraisal sheets, and other materials which for half a century have remained preserved in Washington. Even more thanks are due to William D. Welge, director of the Archives and Manuscripts Division of the Oklahoma Historical Society, who brought to our attention the existence of the large collection of Works Progress Administration Federal Writers' Project slave narratives preserved in the Society's holdings. Without his generous assistance, this publication of the interviews would never have been possible.

Special thanks are due not only to the archivists in Washington, D.C., and Oklahoma City but also to the librarians at the Center for American History at the University of Texas at Austin, where typescripts from the Texas Slave Narrative Project of the Works Progress Administration are held. They assisted not only with our research on the typescripts there but also in providing valuable reference materials used in preparing annotations. Kent Keeth, Michael Toon, Ellen K. Brown, and Eric Morrow at the Texas Collection, Baylor University, played key roles throughout this project in making published and microfilm materials available for the annotations. They also provided scores of books and dozens of reels of microfilm. Thanks, good friends, for the help.

A number of private individuals contributed valuable information on the preparation of annotations for these interviews. We would like to acknowledge particularly the contributions of William W. Gwaltney,

Dr. Bob L. Blackburn, Dr. Rebecca Sharpless, Dr. Thomas L. Charlton, Edward C. Shoemaker, Mrs. Joe T. Craig, Mrs. James W. Ivy, Mr. and Mrs. LeRoy Fowler, Gary Harrington, Robert L. Schaadt, Darlene Mott, David E. Montgomery, Dr. Alwyn Barr, and Skipper Steely. Special thanks go to Dr. James Smallwood and to Dr. Jimmie Lee Franklin, historians on African Americans in Oklahoma, for the insights they shared. Calvin B. Smith, chair of the Department of Museum Studies at Baylor University, and Joel W. Victory III, city manager of Cleburne, Texas, allowed us to have flexible work schedules to undertake research in both Oklahoma and Washington, D.C., and provided constant encouragement for scholarly research.

Our parents, Mr. and Mrs. Garnell A. Baker of Cleburne, Texas, and Col. and Mrs. Julian H. Philips of Houston, Texas, provided particular encouragement and support throughout the preparation of the manuscript.

Special thanks go to George W. Bauer and John N. Drayton, director and editor-in-chief, respectively, at the University of Oklahoma Press, for permitting the Texas A&M University Press to publish the interviews of Texas ex-slaves comprising this work, the texts of which were drawn from a larger study of slave narratives from the Oklahoma Federal Writers' Project published by the University of Oklahoma Press.

This study was supported in part by funds from the Baylor University Research Committee, which facilitated travel to conduct research at the University of Oklahoma libraries in Norman, Oklahoma, at the Historical Society, and at the Oklahoma Division of Libraries in Oklahoma City, Oklahoma.

Introduction

For decades the bondage of black slaves to white masters was a part of everyday life in Texas. As early as the 1820s, settlers from the United States began bringing substantial numbers of African American bondmen and bondwomen to Texas, and by the eve of the Civil War almost one-third of the total Texas population was made up of black slaves. Though Texas in time became identified with western states, for much of the nineteenth century it remained predominately Southern in its mores and ideals. The narratives comprising this book tell about the Texans who lived in servitude during the middle years of the nineteenth century.

Although the shelves of research libraries are laden with the many volumes written on the history of African American slavery, most of these studies have depended on traditional sources, many of which were written by whites, since most slaves were illiterate. Although these traditional sources may indeed be valid, they do not tell the personal stories of the people who lived inside the bonds of the institution—the slaves.

This is not a book about slavery. It is, instead, a book about what it was like to be a slave. The sources for this topic are not letters or account books from white masters; they are the memories of the slaves themselves. They are recollections of being sold away from parents, of living in misery, of suffering the pain of the overseer's lash, and of being the chosen mate of the master. Such remembrances, taken from the transcripts of interviews from the 1930s as part of the Federal Writers' Project, are the life stories of former slaves in Texas who, after freedom, relocated to Oklahoma and were interviewed there.

Slavery, which influenced the lives of virtually every Texan from the 1820s to 1860s, developed in stages over several decades. The first black to arrive in present-day Texas is thought to be the Moor' Esteban, who landed with a party of shipwrecked Spanish explorers off the Texas coast in 1528. But human bondage was almost nonexistent in Spanish Colonial Texas. It was not until several decades later, after the Mexican Revolution of 1821 against Spain, that Stephen F. Austin began the legal settlement of colonists from the United States into Texas. The émigrés from east of the Sabine River, who followed Austin and other land agents, brought with them their black bondmen. By the fall of 1825, Austin's Colony on the lower Brazos River included 443 slaves, nearly a quarter of the total population of approximately 1,800 settlers.

Although Texas and other southern states upheld the institution of slavery, most of the western world had recognized that human bondage was morally wrong. African slave trade had been abolished by most European and New World countries, including the United States. But as late as 1865, the South remained a strong adherent to black slavery.

Mexican authorities generally disapproved of the human bondage which they saw growing in Texas, but they did nothing to abolish the institution. When the State of Coahuila and Texas promulgated a new state constitution in 1827 which prohibited the introduction of new slaves to the state, American immigrants reacted by continuing to bring in blacks, not as slaves but as "indentured servants." Mexican officials ignored the loophole, especially since, under Mexican law, the status for the bondmen was ambiguous. But even though bondmen were considered indentured, English-speaking settlers clearly considered them to be their property.

In 1830 Mexican President Antonio López de Santa Anna issued a decree to deal with what authorities viewed as an unrestricted flow of settlers from the United States into Texas. Because officials had begun doubting the loyalty of non–Spanish-speaking immigrants, the Law of April 6, 1830, prohibited the further entry of Americans or their slaves to Texas. In the face of the government officials' inability to enforce the statutory prohibition, more white settlers with their black bondmen continued to filter into the state.

When revolution broke out between Texan settlers and Mexico in 1835, slavery was not the cause, but it was a contributing influence. Emigrants from the United States understood that, although Mexican authorities had passively opposed slavery, both American state and national governments had passed laws restricting it. When the insurgents gained their victory over Santa Anna at San Jacinto in April, 1836, they won a war fought over many issues, only one of which had been slavery. One of the major consequences of the victory, however, was that the new Republic of Texas secured the institution of slavery for its white citizens and provided it a firm foundation for years to come.

The Texas Republic now formally confirmed slavery as a legal institution. Congress enacted a series of measures, mostly copied from laws in the American South, which dealt with people who were held as private property. These laws guaranteed the right of individuals to own slaves, defined specific criminal acts against slaves (such as mutilation and murder), regulated the conduct of bondmen, addressed problems of retrieving runaway slaves, and defined the status of the few free blacks.

This formal protection of the "peculiar institution" began an era of rapid growth for slavery in the Republic, which continued steadily until emancipation at the end of the Civil War. During the ten years of the Texas Republic, its slave population grew approximately 450 percent, from almost 5,000 to nearly 27,500, a greater rate of growth than for the white population. This trend continued after annexation to the United States in 1845. At the time of the first U.S. census in Texas in 1850, enumerators counted 58,161 slaves out of a total Texas population of 212,592—27.4 percent of the total number of inhabitants. By the next census in 1860, the Texas slave population had grown to 182,566 out of a total of 604,521—30.2 percent of all Texans. Although the population of Texas was growing through immigration and births, the number of slaves was growing at a faster rate only through immigration. Rather than being born in Texas, most of the new bondmen were arriving with their masters from the American South. They shared roots like those of Lamar County ex-slave George W. Harmon, who claimed, "My father came from Tennessee and my mother from Virginia."

Slavery expanded and seemingly prospered in Texas for a number of reasons. The land and climate in the eastern third of the Lone Star State clearly was similar to the American South, making it comparatively easy for settlers owning slaves to move westward to Texas from the South. In leaving behind worn-out lands, resettled Southerners occupied rich soils in the new country, which were well suited to agricultural practices they already knew. The institution of slavery also made the transfer. Black servitude proved to be economically viable. In Texas, land rich but labor poor, owners worked their slaves strenuously and for long hours, earning handsome profits from their slave labor.

Of all the states in the southern Confederacy, Texas suffered the least from military actions. Although some fighting occurred along the Gulf coast and in the lower Rio Grande Valley, no major invasions or destruction of property in Texas took place during the Civil War. Thus, the land and its slaves remained undisturbed.

For this reason, Texas during the war was viewed as a haven for safeguarding the institution of slavery through a system called "refugeeing," which allowed masters to send their bondmen from other southern states to Texas. Because owners feared that Union forces in the South would liberate their slave property, thousands of African Americans trekked with their masters to Texas between 1861 and 1865. A number of Texas ex-slaves who were interviewed in Oklahoma remembered making the trip to Texas during the war. Allen V. Manning, who was refugeed to Coryell County, recalled: "About that time it look like everybody in the world was going to Texas. When we would be going down the road we would have to walk along the side all the time to let the wagons go past, all loaded with folks going to Texas." Mary Lindsay, who was a slave in Fannin County during the war, also remembered that "they was whole families of them with they children and they slaves along, and they was coming in from every place because the Yankees was gitting in their part of the country, they say."

Although only 6 percent of the Texas slaves enumerated in the 1860 census belonged to nonfarmers, over 60 percent belonged to the one-fourth of masters who owned ten or more slaves. Therefore, most of the Texas ex-slave remembrances are of plantation life on commercial farms that raised cash crops like cotton. One-fourth of the white households in Texas owned slaves, the same proportion as in Virginia. The area encompassed by slavery in Texas, the third of the state east of the 98th meridian, was comparable in size to Mississippi and Alabama combined. Clearly, Texas was a major slave state where slavery indeed was an important part of life for many Texans.

Since most Texas blacks lived on plantations, their annual work routine was dictated by the seasonal cycle of planting, cultivating, and harvesting of crops. Red River Valley ex-slave Sonny Greer described a typical day thus: "Start to work at daylight and quit when the sun went down." Phyllis Petite, a former slave in Rusk County, recalled: "That old horn blowed 'way before daylight, and all the field negroes had to be out in the row by the time of sun up. House negroes got up too, because old Master always up to see everybody get out to work." Allen V. Manning, formerly a slave in Coryell County, claimed his master had been trained from childhood to view his slaves the same way he viewed his draft animals. Manning said, "If they [his slaves] act like they his work hosses they git along all right. But if they don't—Oh, oh!"

The work week for most Texas field workers included time off on Sundays, but on other days slaves generally knew only continuous work. Most masters recognized Christmas as a holiday and sometimes gave their bondmen as much as a week off during the nongrowing season. According to Sonny Greer: "Christmas time wasn't much different [than] any other, except if it come in the middle of the week we get the rest of the week to ourselves. Just take care of the light chores. If Christmas come on Saturday then we had to be ready for work on the next Monday." Other masters were not as generous with holidays, and Bob Maynard, formerly in servitude in Falls County, said, "Sunday was our only day for recreation."

Although some masters hired white overseers to manage their agricultural operations, others designated individual slaves as black drivers or overseers. Often despised by the other bondmen, these men found themselves in the awkward position of having to ensure that the work ordered by the master was done by the slaves. Lou Smith told her interviewer: "Old Master was his own overseer, but my daddy was the overlooker. He was purty hard on them too, as they had to work just like they never got tired." Mollie Watson from Leon County related that on her master's plantation "nigger drivers was de cullud overseers. Dey sho' was mean. Dey was so biggety an' such smart-alexs an' dey worked de niggers so hard dat all de hands hated 'em." One of these black drivers finally went too far, according to Watson. "Once Marse Bastian had a cullud overseer dat was allus beatin' on some one and one day all de hands ganged up on him an' beat him till he died."

Because the plantations required more than just field labor, many slaves became skilled artisans, some of them using those skills after gaining freedom and becoming independent businessmen. Alice Rawlings told her interviewer that her father was a blacksmith on the plantation in Cass County and was "the hardest working slave on Major Jackson's Texas plantation." She added that "even before the slaves was made free my father earned outside money that his master allowed him to keep."

A smaller proportion of slaves worked within the households of white masters and mistresses, and though their labor may have been less arduous, they worked under the closer scrutiny of white owners. But their work hours were not necessarily shorter. Johnson Thompson remembered from his boyhood in Rusk County: "Mammy was the house girl and she weaved the cloth and my Aunt 'Tilda dyed the cloth with wild indigo, leaving her hands blue looking most of the time. Mammy work late in the night, and I hear the loom making noises while I try to sleep in the cabin." Household slaves often prepared meals for white masters, which enabled the cooks to eat better food than the other slaves. But they, too, often paid a price by being criticized by the whites for the slightest problems in the kitchen. John White, who cooked and washed for his white master and mistress in Cass County, took advantage of his master's sometimes skimpy rationing of food to the field hands this way: "Sometimes they'd borrow, sometimes I'd slip somethings from out the kitchen. The single women folks was bad that way. I favors them with something extra from the kitchen. Then they favors me—at night when the overseer thinks everybody asleep in they own places!"

In most instances Texas slaves received adequate amounts of nourishment, as it was in the interests of the owners to keep their slaves healthy and strong enough to work. For the most part the blacks and whites shared basically similar diets heavy in pork, corn, and molasses. Typically, masters rationed out raw food by the week, as Bob Maynard remembered from his days in servitude: "Old Master raised hundreds of hogs; he raised practically all the food we et. He gave the food out to each family and they done their own cooking except during harvest." Frequently masters had black cooks prepare midday meals for slave children, as Francis [Frances] Bridges remembered from her days in bondage in Red River County: "The cook, Mama Winnie Long, used to feed all us little niggers on the flo', jest like little pigs, in tin cups and wooden spoons." Lizzie Farmer, of Mount Enterprise, Texas, shared fond memories of meals on the John Booker plantation: "When we went to cook our vegetables we would put a big piece of hog jowl in de pot. We'd put in a lot of snap beans and when dey was about half done we'd put in a mess of cabbage and when it was about half done we'd put in some squash and when it was about half done we'd put in some okra. Then when it was done we would take it out a layer at a time. Go 'way! It makes me hungry to talk about it."

Housing for Texas slaves was rude at best. Modest cabins provided shelter from the elements, but they were hot and stuffy during the summertime and cold and drafty during the winter. Eliza Elsey, who lived near Plantersville in Grimes County, told her interviewer: "I know about the slave cabins; they was all set in a long row, and . . . made of logs. There was a fireplace made of mud, and the dirt floor was rock hard from all the feets that tramp over it all the time. The cabins all alike, one room with a door, but no windows."

Clothing for Texas slaves was inexpensive and durable, its fabric often handwoven in the rural households, but frequently it was barely adequate. Annie Hawkins's remembrances of women's and girls' garments were that "our dresses was made out of coarse cloth like cotton sacking and it sho' lasted a long time. It ort to been called mule-hide for it was about that tough." Mollie Watson, who lived and worked at a tavern and livery stable on the courthouse square in Centerville, related that her mistress gave the women slaves her worn-out garments "to dress up in." Men typically wore coarse fabric trousers, shirts, and jackets, but boys wore long-tailed loose-fitting shirts until their teenage years. Red Richardson, who grew up as a child slave wearing long-tailed shirts in Grimes County, told his interviewer many years later, "I didn't know what pants was until I was 14."

Most bondmen received medical attention from white physicians if they were seriously ill or badly injured. Unfortunately, even the best white physicians did not necessarily provide the best care. After Fannin County slave Mary Lindsay broke her arm in the 1860s, her mistress called for a doctor to treat the injury, but the girl suffered a relapse. "My broke arm begin to swell up and hurt me, and I git sick with it again," she remembered.

"Mistress git another doctor to come and look at it. He say I got bad blood from it how come I git so sick, and he git out his knife out'n his satchel and bleed me in the other arm." The next day the doctor returned "and bleed me again two times, and the next day one more time, and then I git so sick I puke and he quit bleeding me." Eventually she recovered without further medical attention. In addition to visits from white physicians, many African Americans practiced folk cures for illnesses. Eliza Elsey, from Grimes County, Texas, related, "When the Negro babies cry with the stomach ache they give them hen feathers tea, and when they break out with the hives, there was nothing better than sheep wool tea."

Masters of Texas slaves ranged from humane to brutal. Slaves had to suffer the whims of their master's anger with little recourse. Acemy Wofford remembered this incident from her slavery days in Texas: "When the mistress got mad, and that was likely to happen most any time, the slaves got pretty rough handling. She would pick up anything close and let it fly. Buckets or stone jars, sticks or boards, didn't make no difference, just so's it was loose." Although some masters and bondmen shared a genuine fondness for each other, many slaves assumed the appearance of affection in order to get along with the domineering whites. But most Texas slaves experienced lives shaded by ill treatment from their owners. Annie Hawkins, who came from Georgia to Texas with her master's household, had little good to say about the master class: "I never had no whitefolks that was good to me. We all worked jest like dogs and had about half enough to eat and got whupped for everything. Our days was a constant misery to us. I know lots of niggers that was slaves had a good time but we never did. Seems hard that I can't say anything good for any of 'em, but I sho' can't."

Physical punishment and fear of punishment cast dark shadows across the lives of many Texas slaves. Ida Henry, a native of Marshall, Texas, later recounted an incident from her childhood which remained as vivid in her memory during her summer, 1937, interview as when she witnessed it over seventy years before. Her mother, a very religious person, was praying outside her quarters at night, when she was approached by members of the white slave patrol. When they discovered that she did not have a written pass from her master permitting her to be out at night, according to Henry, "dey stripped her naked and tied her hands together and wid a rope tied to de hand cuffs and threw one end of de rope over a limb and tied de other end to de pommel of a saddle on a horse." She continued, "Dey pulled her up so dat her toes could barely touch de ground and whipped her."

Some of the most vivid memories from slavery days in Texas are of the bullwhip and what it did to human flesh. John White, a slave in Cass

County, described one of his encounters with the lash in the hands of his master, Presley Davenport. As a house servant, White washed clothes as well as cooked for the Davenport household. On one occasion he inadvertently left a soapy streak in one of his master's shirts:

> *I learns to be careful about streaks in the clothes. I learns by the bull whip. One day the Master finds a soapy streak in his shirt. Then he finds me.*
>
> *The Military Road goes by the place and the Master drives me down the road and ties me to a tree. First he tears off the old shirt and then he throws the bull whip to me. When he is tired of beating me more torture is a-coming. The salt water cure. It don't cure nothing but that's what the white folks called it. "Here's at you," the Master say, and slap the salt water into the bleeding cuts. "Here's at you!" The blisters burst every time he slap me with the brine.*
>
> *Then I was loosened to stagger back into the kitchen. The Mistress couldn't do nothing about it 'cept to lay on the grease thick, with a kind word to help stop the misery.*

In the face of experiences such as these, the family served as a sustaining influence in the lives of many Texas slaves. The families provided essential emotional and mental strength for their members. Andrew Simms, a slave in Freestone County, told the following story about his parents' meeting. "Somehow or other mammy and pappy meets 'round the place and the first thing happens they is in love. That's what mammy see. And the next thing that happen is me." The slave families offered the children both love and discipline. Noah Perry related that on one occasion when he was growing up, a slave man on the plantation gave him a whipping for doing something wrong. Perry told his mother about it when she returned home from a day in the fields, and she followed the man "to the barn . . . and drug him out and gave him a good thrashing." That was not all, however, for then she returned to the cabin and "spanked us good and proper" for the infraction. Such love punctuated with discipline clearly provided emotional support for many members of black families in the face of harsh situations beyond their control.

Since slave families had no standing before the law in Texas, owners often thoughtlessly separated family members through sales, gifts, bequests, and even debt settlements. Growing up in Centerville, Mollie Watson viewed slave auctions on the courthouse square in the town. She later reported to her interviewer that "speclators uster buy up niggers jest lak dey was animals. . . . Dey . . . would parade 'em round town an' den take 'em to de town square an' put 'em on de block an' sell 'em. I've seen men, wives an' little chillen sold away from each other." Lou Smith's family was separated as a result of her master's default on a loan. "My father belonged to Huriah Longacre," she said. "He put up a lot of his slaves as security on a debt and he took sick and died so they put them all on de block and sold them." Phyllis Petite's husband had been separated from his mother by sale when he was just a boy. When the new owner took the mother away from the child, according to Petite, the child "looked down a long lane after her just as long as he could see her, and cried after her. He went down to the big road and set down by his mammy's barefooted tracks in the sand and set there until it got dark, and then he come on back to the quarters." He never saw his mother again. Some family units were the result of the master's wishes. Eliza Elsey reported that on the plantation where she lived in Grimes County, "Old Master Tom Smith . . . treated his slaves like animals. He take the strongest men and women, put them together in a cabin so's they raise him some more husky children."

Religion provided a source of strength for Texans living in bondage. Not only did religious services provide an emotional release, but belief in salvation gave them hope that the afterlife would be happier. Bob Maynard remembered that on Sundays in Falls County "we went to church at our own church and we could sing and shout jest as loud as we pleased and it didn't disturb nobody." On other plantations the owners controlled the services, using religion as a means of manipulating their slaves' behavior. Ida Henry said that in Harrison County "on Sunday mornings before breakfast our Mistress would call us together, read de Bible and show us pictures of de Devil in de Bible and tell us dat if we was not good and if we would steal and tell lies dat old Satan would git us." But left on their own, John White said that in Cass County, where he lived, the slaves would meet on Sundays and "pray for to get out of bondage."

Music provided a means for self-expression and diversion that helped many Texas slaves survive the psychological assaults of slavery. From her childhood in servitude in Centerville, Mollie Watson remembered that since her Aunt Luce had a larger cabin than the other slaves, the master allowed them to dance there. And, according to Bob Maynard, "after supper we would all set round the doors outside and sing or play music." He went on to add: "The only musical instruments we had was a jug or a big bottle, a skillet lid or frying pan that they'd hit with a stick or a bone. We had a flute too, made out of reed cane and it'd make good music. Sometimes we'd sing and dance so long and loud old Master'd have to make us stop and go to bed." The music, both secular and religious, reflected the slaves' frustrations with their lives. Harriett Robinson recited the words that went with a fiddle tune she remembered from growing up in Bastrop County:

I fooled Old Mastah 7 years
Fooled the overseer three;
Hand me down my banjo
And I'll tickle your bel-lee.

Slaves in Texas as elsewhere in the South responded to their situations in a range of ways. At one extreme were the bondsmen who surrendered completely, identifying with their masters and their families to the exclusion of other slaves. At the opposite pole were individuals who resisted the institution in every way that they could. Most of the bondsmen responded to their situations in ways somewhere between these two extremes. Although the blacks realized that they were not in control of the world in which they found themselves, they still attempted to influence it any way they could.

Masters constantly reinforced the idea that whites held total control over their slaves. Annie Hawkins explained to her interviewer, "You must remember he owned us body and soul and they wasn't anything we could do about it." And seemingly unrelated events served as opportunities to remind slaves of their subservience. Harriett Robinson said that "when-ever white folks had a baby born den all de old niggers had to come thoo the room and the master would be over 'hind the bed and he'd say, 'Here's a new little mistress or master you got to work for.' You had to say, 'Yessuh Master' and bow real low or the overseer would crack you."

Despite the masters' lessons, slaves often exercised some creative forms of resistance. For example, Phyllis Petite said black adults actively com-municated with bondmen on other plantations. "We used to carry news from one plantation to the other," she stated, "'cause mammy would tell about things going on some other plantation and I know she never been there." Petty thievery provided a means for Marshall native Ida Henry to strike back at her masters. While working at the "big house," she "would put biscuits and pieces of chicken in a sack under me dress dat hung from me waist, as I waited de table for me Mistress, and later would slip off and eat it as dey never gave de slaves none of dis sort of food." Annie Hawkins remembered one incident that took place following the death of her mas-ter, who habitually abused alcohol. "He finally killed hisself drinking and I remember Old Mistress called us in to look at him in his coffin," she told her interviewer. "We all marched by him slow like and I jest hap-pened to look up and caught my sister's eye and we both jest natchelly laughed—Why shouldn't we? We was glad he was dead. It's a good thing we had our laugh fer old Mistress took us out and whupped us with a broomstick."

A substantial number of blacks resisted slavery more overtly by running away. Some bondmen enjoyed a brief respite by escaping to the woods for a few days of freedom before returning to their families on the plantations. After Easter Wells's mother, a cook on a Brazos Valley plantation, had burned the bread for the white family, she ran off to the woods because she could not face the punishment—having to eat all the scorched loaves. For days she hid in the woods, surviving by having another slave slip food out to her, but after two weeks she returned. Wells remembered: "Finally she come home and old Master give her a whipping but he didn't hurt her none. He was glad to git her back." Her mother explained to her family and friends that "she could'a slipped off to de North but she didn't want to leave us children. She was afraid young Master would be mad and sell us and we'd a-had a hard time so she come back."

Some slaves, like Harriett Robinson's stepfather, Uncle Isom, in Bastrop County, were persistent runaways, but he was also "a double-strengthened man":

> He'd run off so help you God. They had the blood hounds after him once and he caught the hound what was leading and beat the rest of the dogs. The white folks run up on him before he knowed it and made them dogs eat his ear plumb out. But don't you know he got away anyhow. One morning I was sweeping out the hall in the big house and somebody come a-knocking on the front door and I goes to the door. There was Uncle Isom wid rags all on his head. He said, "Tell old master heah I am." I goes to Master's door and says, "Master Colonel Sam, Uncle Isom said heah eh am." He say, "[Well, well, Mr. Isom, thought you was dead.] Go 'round to the kitchen and tell black mammy to give you breakfast." When he was thoo eating they give him 300 lashes and, bless my soul, he run off again.

Occasionally violence erupted, as when a white overseer threatened to shoot Alice Rawlings's mother. "She grabbed the gun and run for the river," Rawlings reported, but "she dropped the gun in the river and the overseer got over his temper and left her alone." But such encounters often ended with more serious consequences. After the Civil War began, Ida Henry's master went into the army, so the white overseer "tried himself in meanness over de slaves as seemingly he tried to be important." The result was that "one day de slaves caught him and one held him whilst another knocked him in the head and killed him." Lewis Bonner's father, also a runaway, reportedly killed several white slave patrol members who tried to capture him. Although the number he killed was exaggerated, the story illustrates well the feelings of resistance that existed just below the surface of outward subservience.

Freedom finally came to Texas slaves, not on April 21, 1865, when Robert E. Lee surrendered to Ulysses S. Grant at Appomattox Courthouse, but nearly two months later. The time it took Union military forces to occupy Texas after the Confederate surrender accounted for the delay. On June 19, 1865, Union General Gordon Granger, commander of federal occupation forces in Galveston, formally announced the emancipation proclamation in Texas, signaling the end of slavery in the state. "The night peace was told me," Acemy Wofford remembered, "I prayed to the Lord. I was thankful." Lou Smith, child slave of an abusive mistress in Texas, was eleven years old when she learned of her freedom: "I ran off and hid in the plum orchard and said over'n over, 'I'se free, I'se free; I ain't never going back to Miss Jo.'" The response Phyllis Petite observed among the slaves on the plantation where she lived in Rusk County was a familiar one, though repeated in different words and with varying details by many of the interviewees: "One day old Master stay after he eat breakfast and when us negroes come in to eat he say: 'After today I ain't your master any more. You all as free as I am.' We just stand and look and don't know what to say about it." Indeed many slaves did not know how to react to the news that they were free, that for the first time they would become their own masters, and that they would now make decisions about their own lives.

Not all masters informed their bondmen of their freedom. Amanda Oliver, in servitude in a household on the outskirts of Sherman, remembered: "Old Mistress didn't tell us when we was free, but another white woman told my mother . . . I remembuh one day old mistress told my mother to git to that [spinning] wheel and git to work, and my mother said, 'I ain't gwineter, I'm just as free as you air.' So dat very day my mother packed up all our belongings and moved us to town."

Slavery, at one time a way of life for almost one-third of all Texans, is retold in the interviews that follow. These narratives tell how Texas slaves dealt with daily life in which they found themselves treated more like animals than as humans. They also tell about the resilience of the human spirit, a resilience that has expressed itself in different ways and in different words by oppressed people around the world. It happens, however, that these are the stories of Texans.

Till Freedom Cried Out

L. B. Barner/Lewis Bonner

❦ ❦ ❦

Age Unknown
Anderson County

L. B. BARNER

I's born in Palestine Texas. I don't know how old I is. I was 9 years old when freedom cried out.

My father was name Kater Barner after master Mat Swanson and my mothers name Amy Swanson. My father wouldn't work and just scouted through the woods. One day they decided to catch him and he ran into the woods and when they had ran him down he killed 18 white men or patrollers.

I have 2 brothers (he says, "me and my brother") and one sister.

As a child I played in the quarters during the day and did a little work for my mistress such as churning and many nights after staying at my mistress house later at nights I would sleep across the foot of her bed at her feet. My mother plowed a brown mule and that mule had so much sense all you had to do was turn that mule out and he would go to the field and back up to the right plow and wait until my mother got there to hitch him up.

As a slave I ate at my masters house and I waited on the table and fanned the flies. In hot weather we wore a long shirt but in winter we wore jean pants and shoes made on the plantation.

My master and mistress was good to their slaves. He never whipped his slaves unless he caught one of them in a lie as they gave them no trouble and worked hard. They had one child girl name Julia. Their house was a 3 room house on the plantation. The overseer was a Negro who would tell them each morning what to do and as my master had so many hogs and cattle Unkle [*sic*] John the overseer would send the work hands to the field and he would go look up the hogs and cattle as they ran wild in the woods and feed them corn, etc.

My master owned a large amount of land and between 400 and 500 slaves including children. At 4 o'clock the Negro overseer would awake the slaves for their breakfast as they cooked for themselves. One Negro lady (Aunt Claridy) stayed in the quarters and cook for the 150 or more Negro slave children and also worked around for the mistress during the other part of the day.

On Saturday's and Sunday's the slaves would have church in the quarters. There were 3 or 4 preachers among them but preacher John Swanson was thought the favorite and best.

The patrollers traveled from plantation to plantation during the nights with dogs, guns and bull whips. They would sick [*sic*] the hounds on the slaves and when they would climb a tree they would, if slave was mean[,] climb tree and knock him out and the dogs would sometime tare [*sic*] him up before they could get them of[f] him, or else if he would come down at their demand they would whip him so that he would be unable to work and that is how the master would know they were caught out at nights.

On Christmas and New Years our master would buy barrels of whiskey at the end of the harvests and on these two holidays call the slaves up to the big house and give them all they could drink untill some would become drunk.

The slaves also would carry plenty pep[p]er with them to rub on the bottom of their feet at nights when they slipped of[f] so that the dogs couldn't scent them. The pep[p]er would go up the dogs nose so that they could not track them.

When a slave got sick Dr. Link would come to them and give them calomel and pills. The slaves would keep asafetida around the children's neck to keep them from having the [w]hooping-cough, etc.

Just before the [Civil] war started some of the Negro slaves went to build bre[a]st works and returned and the next day war broke out.

When master notified or told his slaves that they were free he told them "you are free now just like I am and as you have no places to go you can remain in the quarters untill you see fit to go."

My wife was name Lizzie Billinger and have 4 girls and 2 boys and 11 grandchildren.

"I think Abraham Lincoln much of a man. My pick."

"Now that slavery is over I don't care to go in it any more. I would fight first."

LEWIS BONNER

I was born 7 miles north of Palestine, Texas on Matt Swanson's place in 1850, but I kin not remember the date. My mistress was name Celia Swanson. My mistress was so good to me till I jest loved her.

My family and all slaves on our place was treated good. Mighty few floggings went on round and about. Master was the overseer over his darkies and didn't use no other'n. I waited table and churned in the Big House.

I ate at the table with my mistress and her family and nothing was evah said. We ate bacon, greens, Irish potatoes and such as we git now. Aunt Chaddy was the cook and nurse for all the chillun on the place.

We used to hear slaves on de other places hollering from whippings, but master never whipped his niggers 'less they lied. Sometimes slaves from other places would run off and come to our place. Master would take them back and tell the slave-holders how to treat them so dey wouldn't run off again.

Mistress had a little stool for me in the big house, and if I got sleepy, she put me on the foot of her bed and I stayed there til [*sic*] morning, got up washed my face and hands and got ready to wait on the table.

There was four or five hundred slaves on our place. One morning during slavery, my father killed 18 white men and ran away. They said he was lazy and whipped him, and he just killed all of 'em he could, which was 18 of 'em. He stayed away 3 years without being found. He come back and killed 7 before they could kill him. When he was on the place he jest made bluing.

My mother worked in the field and weaved cloth. Shirts dat she made lasted 12 months, even if wore and washed and ironed every day. Pants could not be ripped with two men pulling on dem with all their might. You talking 'bout clothes, them was some clothes then. Clothes made now jest don't come up to them near abouts.

Doing of [*sic*] slavery, we had the best church, lots better than today. I am a Baptist from head to foot, yes sir, yes sir. Jest couldn't be nothing else. In the first place, I wouldn't even try.

I knows when the war started and ceaseted. I tell you it was some war. When it was all over, the Yankees came thoo' singing, "You may die poor but you won't die a slave."

When the War was over, master told us that we could go out and take care of the crops already planted and plant the ones that need planting 'cause we knowed all 'bout the place and we would go halvers. We stayed on 3 years after slavery. We got a little money, but we got room and board and didn't have to work too hard. It was enough difference to tell you was no slaves any more.

After slavery and when I was old enough I got married. I married a gal that was a daughter of her master. He wanted to own her, but she sho' didn't return it. He kept up with her till he died and sent her money jest all the time. Before he died, he put her name in his will and told his oldest son to be sure and keep up with her. The son was sure true to his promise, for till she died, she was forever hearing from him or he would visit us, even after we moved to Oklahoma from Texas.

Our chillun and grandchillun will git her part since she is gone. She was sure a good wife and for no reason did I take the second look at no woman. That was love, which don't live no more in our hearts.

I make a few pennies selling fish worms and doing a little yard work and raising vegetables. Not much money in circulation. When I gets my old age pension, it will make things a little mite better. I guess the time will be soon.

Tain't nothing but bad treatment that makes people die young and I ain't had none.

Francis [Frances] Bridges

❦ ❦ ❦

Age 73 Years
Red River County

I was born in Red River County, Texas in 1864, and that makes me 73 years old. I had myself 75, and I went to my white folks and they counted it up and told me I was 73, but I always felt like I was older than that.

My husband's name is Henry Bridges. We was raised up children together and married. I had five sisters. My brother died here in Oklahoma about two years ago. He was a Fisher. Mary Russell, my sister, she lives in Parish [Paris], Texas; Willie Ann Poke, she lives in Greenville, Texas; Winnie Jackson, lives in Adonia [Ladonia], Texas, and Mattie White, my other sister, lives in Long Oak [Lone Oak], Texas, White Hunt County.

Our master was named Master Travis Wright, and we all ate nearly the same thing. Such things as barbecued rabbits, coon, possums baked with sweet potatoes and all such as that. I used to hang round the kitchen. The cook, Mama Winnie Long, used to feed all us little niggers on the flo', jest like little pigs, in tin cups and wooden spoons. We ate fish too, and I like to go fishing right this very day.

We lived right in old Master Wright's yard. His house sat way up on a high hill. It was jest a little old log hut we lived in[,] a little old shack around the yard. They was a lot of little shacks in the yard, I can't tell jest how many, but it was quite a number of 'em. We slept in old-fashion beds that we called "corded beds," 'cause they had ropes crossed to hold the mattresses for slats. Some of 'em had beds nailed to the wall.

Master Travis Wright had one son named Sam Wright, and after old Master Travis Wright died, young Master Sam Wright come to be my mother's master. He jest died a few years ago.

My mother say dey had a nigger driver and he'd whip 'em all but his daughter. I never seen no slaves whipped, but my mother say dey had to whip her Uncle Charles Mills once for tell a story. She say he bored a hole in de wall of de store 'till he bored de hole in old Master's whiskey barrel, and he caught two jugs of whiskey and buried it in de banks of de river. When old Master found out de whiskey was gone, he tried to make Uncle

Charley 'fess up, and Uncle Charley wouldn't so he brung him in and hung him and barely let his toes touch. After Uncle Charley thought he was going to kill him, he told where de whiskey was.

We didn't go to church before freedom, land no! 'cause the closest church was so far—it was 30 miles off. But I'm a member of the Baptist Church and I've been a member for some 40-odd years. I was past 40 when I heerd of a Methodist Church. My favorite song is "Companion." I didn't get to go to school 'till after slavery.

I 'member more after de War. I 'member my mother said dey had patrollers, and if de slaves would get passes from de Master to go to de dances and didn't git back before ten o'clock dey'd beat 'em half to death.

I used to hear 'em talking 'bout Ku Klux Klan coming to the well to get water. They'd draw up a bucket of water and pour the water in they false stomachs. They false stomachs was tied on 'em with a big leather buckle. They'd jest pour de water in there to scare 'em and say, "This is the first drink of water I've had since I left Hell." They'd say all sech things to scare the cullud folks.

I heerd my mother say they sold slaves on what they called an auction

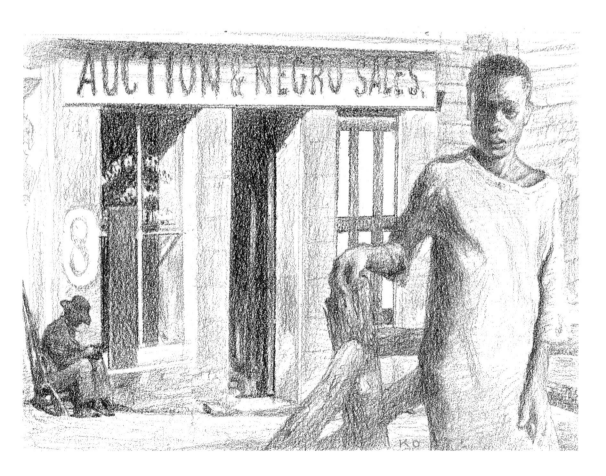

block. Jest like if a slave had any portly fine looking children they'd sell them chillun jest like selling cattle. I didn't see this, jest heerd it.

After freedom, when I was old enough to work in the field, we lived on Mr. Martin's plantation. We worked awful hard in the fields. Lawd yes'm! I've heard 'bout shucking up de corn, but give me dem cotton pickings. Fry'd [Dey'd] pick out all de crop of cotton in one day. The women would cook and de men'd pick the cotton, I mean on dem big cotton pickings. Some would work for they meals. Then after dey'd gather all de crops, dey's give big dances, drink whiskey, and jest cut up sumpin terrible. We didn't know anything 'bout holidays.

I've heard my husband talk 'bout "Raw head an' bloody bones." Said whenever dey mothers wanted to scare 'em to make 'em be good dey'd tell 'em dat a man was outside de door and asked her if she'd hold his head while he fixed his back bone. I don't believe in voodooing, and I don't believe in hants. I used to believe in both of 'em when I was young.

I married Jake Bridges. We had an ordinary wedding. The preacher married us and we had a license. We have two sons grown living here. My husband told me that in slavery if your Master told you to live with your brother, you had to live with him. My father's mother and dad was first cousins.

I can 'member my husband telling me he was hauling lumber from Jefferson where the saw mill was and it was cold that night, and when they got halfway back it snowed, and he stopped with an old cullud family, and he said way in the night, a knock come at de door—woke 'em up, and it was an old cullud man, and he said dis old man commence inquiring, trying to find out who dey people was and dey told him best dey could remember, and bless de Lawd, 'fore dey finished talking dey found out dis old cullud man and de other cullud woman an' man dat was married was all brothers and sisters, and he told his brother it was a shame he had married his sister and dey had nine chillun. My husband sho' told me dis.

I've heerd 'em say dey old master raised chillun by those cullud women. Why, there was one white man in Texas had a cullud woman, but didn't have no chillun by her, and had this cullud woman and her old mistress there on the same place. So, when old Mistress died he wouldn't let this cullud woman leave, and he gave her a swell home right there on the place, and she is still there I guess. They say she say sometime, she didn't want no Negro man smutting her sheets up.

I think Abraham Lincoln was a good man, and I have read a whole lots 'bout him, but I don't know much 'bout Jeff Davis. I think Booker T. Washington is a fine man, but I aint heerd so much about him.

Esther Easter

☙ ☙ ☙

Age 85 Years
Fannin County

I was born near Memphis, Tenn., on the old Ben Moore plantation, but I don't know anything about the Old South because Master Ben moves us all up into Missouri (about 14-miles east of Westport, now Kansas City), long before they started fighting about slavery.

Mary Collier was my mother's name before she was a Moore. About my father, I dunno. Mammy was sickly most of the time when I was a baby, and she was so thin and poorly when they move to Missouri the white folks afraid she going die on the way.

But she fool 'em, and she live two-three year after that. That's what good Old Master Ben tells me when I gets older.

I stay with Master Ben's married daughter, Mary, till the coming of the War. Times was good before the War, and I wasn't suffering none from slavery, except once in a while the Mistress would fan me with the stick—bet I needed it, too.

When the War come along Master he say to leave Mistress Mary and get ready to go to Texas. Jim Moore, one of the meanest men I ever see, was the son of Master Ben; he's going take us there.

Demon Jim, that's what I call him when he ain't round the place, but when he's home it was always Master Jim 'cause he was reckless with the whip. He was a Rebel officer fighting round the country and didn't take us slaves to Texas right away. So I stayed on at his place not far from Master Ben's plantation.

Master Jim's wife was a demon, just like her husband. Used the whip all the time, and every time Master Jim come home he whip me 'cause the Mistress say I been mean.

One time I tell him, you better put me in your pocket (sell me), Master Jim, else I'se going run away. He don't pay no mind, and I don't try to run away 'cause of the whips.

I done see one whipping and that enough. They wasn't no fooling about it. A runaway slave from the Jenkin's plantation was brought back,

and there was a public whipping, so's the slaves could see what happens when they tries to get away.

The runaway was chained to the whipping post, and I was full of misery when I see the lash cutting deep into that boy's skin. He swell up like a dead horse, but he gets over it, only he was never no count for work no more.

While Master Jim is out fighting the Yanks, the Mistress is fiddling round with a neighbor man, Mister Headsmith. I is young then, but I knows enough that Master Jim's going be mighty mad when he hears about it.

The Mistress didn't know I knows her secret, and I'm fixing to even up for some of them whippings she put off on me. That's why I tell Master Jim next time he come home.

See that crack in the wall? Master Jim say yes, and I say, it's just like the open door when the eyes are close to the wall. He peek and see into the bedroom.

That's how I find out about the Mistress and Mister Headsmith, I tells him, and I see he's getting mad.

What you mean? And Master Jim grabs me hard by the arm like I was trying to get away.

I see them in the bed.

That's all I say. The Demon's got him and Master Jim tears out of the room looking for the Mistress.

Then I hears loud talking and pretty soon the Mistress is screaming and calling for help, and if old Master Ben hadn't drop in just then and stop the fight, why, I guess she be beat almost to death, that how mad the Master was.

Then Master Ben gets mad 'cause his boy Jim ain't got us down in Texas yet. Then we stay up all the night packing for the trip. Master Jim takes us, but the Mistress stay at home, and I wonder if Master Jim beat her again when he gets back.

We rides the wagons all the way, how many days, I dunno. The country was wild most of the way, and I know now that we come through the same country where I lives now, only it was to the east. (The trip was evidently made over the "Texas Road.") And we keeps on riding and comes to the big river that's all brown and red looking, (Red River) and the next thing I was sold to Mrs. Vaughn at Bonham, Texas, and there I stays till after the slaves is free.

The new Mistress was a widow, no children round the place, and she treat me mighty good. She was good white folks—like old Master Ben, powerful good.

When the word get to us that the slaves is free, the Mistress says I is free to go anywheres I want. And I tell her this talk about being free sounds like foolishment to me—anyway, where can I go? She just pat me on the shoulder and say I better stay right there with her, and that's what I do for a long time. Then I hears about how the white folks down at Dallas pays big money for house girls and there I goes.

That's all I ever do after that—work at the houses till I gets too old to hobble on these tired old feets and legs, then I just sits down.

Just sits down and wishes for old Master Ben to come and get me, and take care of this old woman like he use to do when she is just a little black child on the plantation in Missouri!

God Bless old Master Ben—he was good white folks!

Eliza Elsey

☙ ☙ ☙

Age 77 Years
Grimes County

I aint sure how old I is, but mamma says I was born during the middle of the War, in fodder time. That means in August, 'cause that's when fodder pulling was done, and how come I was born is this way:

Old Master Tom Smith, he the one who own that big plantation, maybe 600 acres, down south in Plantersville, Grimes County, Texas, treated his slaves like animals. He take the strongest men and women, put them together in a cabin so's they raise him some more husky children. That's the kind of a child I is, and that's why I is so big and so healthy at my old age. I weighs about 250 pounds, and I'm 'most 78.

I don't know about my pappy, 'cept mamma say his name was Tom McGowan. My mamma come from North Carolina and work in the fields for old Tom Smith who raised lots of figs and cane and some kind of grapes they call "cut throats." Soon as I is born she go back to the field work, and sometime she feel so bad they whipped her for not working hard enough. She had scars on her back until she died; I see them lots of times and feel sorry that she lived in slave times.

After the War a man named Harrison Sheppard married my mamma and she change her name to Jane Smith Sheppard. They give me three half brothers; Cicero, Jim and George, and four half sisters; Alice, Nessie, Manda and Friona. They are all dead.

The only white child on the plantation was Molly, and she the daughter of Tom Smith and his wife, who lived in a big, fine white plank house, with two chimneys, double. The field hands was never allowed to come into the Master's house, and I don't know how it was fix up.

I know about the slave cabins; they was all set in a long row, and seems like they be a mile long and made of logs. There was a fireplace made of mud, and the dirt floor was rock hard from all the feets that tramp over it all the time. The cabins all alike, one room with a door, but no windows, and mamma say the room was horrible hot in the summer.

All the clothes was made of cotton cloth, even in the winter. That alright for it don't stay cold long, not down south where the sugar cane grow. When a "norther" come the slaves maybe find some old pieces of shoes or wrap up the feets in sacks; if they couldn't find nothing to wear they would work anyways, building a fire with the brush to keep warm by, but they couldn't stay by that fire too much else they get flogged by the overseer that mamma said was the worse one she ever heard of.

The Master ration out the food by the week, and should anybody eat too much they most likely starve before next ration day. Else they steals from each other, or the Master would lose a hog some night when it be darkest. Like the story my mamma told about the slave who got caught under a hog.

The colored man he got hungry, and his little girl Caroline got hungry too, so he takes her with him one night to watch out for the Master while he steal a hog. He kill the hog alright and put him on his back to carry to his cabin, but somehow he stumble in the dark and the dead hog so heavy the girl can't get him off her pappy. Caroline get scared and yell, louder all the time, till the Master come to see about the trouble. He whipped the slave for stealing and the man went hungry waiting for the next rations.

Mamma told me about another time when two men went out to kill a

hog. The hogs root around and sleep under the barn, so one man was to chase them out and the other man was to knock one in the head when he scoot out from under the barn. The hogs run out the other side of the barn, but the Negro come back out the same way he went in and when he stick his head out the man waiting for a hog crack him between the eyes and lay him out. The man died and Master sold the other one to some far off plantation.

Mother always said that stealing in slave days made a birthmark on the younger generation—that's why colored boys and girls steal today.

The Master kept a doctor around most of the time to look after the slaves. He dose out castor oil and turpentine, calomel and blue-mass pills. The children had some little sacks tied around their necks; I know now it was assafetida [*sic*], and it keep off the disease.

When the Negro babies cry with the stomach ache they give them hen feathers tea, and when they break out with the hives, there was nothing better than sheep wool tea.

Some of the slaves didn't believe it when they was freed, and they didn't want to leave the plantation. Whole lots of them kept on working just the same, but they was treated better. They didn't know how to sell cattle or hogs, or sugar cane, and the Master sell part of the crops and give the Negroes some of the money.

After mamma married Harrison Sheppard they move up here to Fort Gibson and I been here since then. I been married three times. First to Bill White, then to Dennis Beck and then to Robert Elsey. They all dead now, and my three children was from my first husband. Two girls and a boy; Armanda, who I lives with, Bessie and George. There is four grandchildren; Hazel Blaine, Leonard Vann, Odell Little and L. V. Little.

That all I can tell about the slave days, but I is proud we all get out of slavery and I is glad that Lincoln is the one that freed us.

Lizzie Farmer

☙ ☙ ☙

Age 80 Years
Rusk County

AUNT LIZZIE FARMER

In a little two room shack that was formerly used as servants' quarters, and situated in the better residential district of McAlester, lives an old colored woman commonly known as "Aunt Lizzie Farmer." She is physically unable to "work in white folks kitchens" any longer, due to rheumatism, so whiles the time away doing little extra jobs for her friends and neighbors and "praise'n de Lord."

Almost every evening neighbors of "Aunt Lizzie" listen in on her devotional hour, or hours, as they often last from two to three hours. They feel that she is sincere in her religious beliefs as she lives them. If a neighbor or friend is ill, whether they be black or white, "Aunt Lizzie" is the first to lend her assistance. For every good deed that comes to her, she returns two.

"Aunt Lizzie" was born near Mount Enterprise Texas in 1861. Her mother having passed away while she was only a year old, she was sent to live with her grandparents, George A. English, and family[,] who were slaves of J. Booker, a plantation holder, however, her grandfather was the "mainest boss" next to Ol' Massa, over the two hundred slaves. Her grandmother Harriet English was born in Eufaula, Oklahoma, about 1827, and was one-half Creek Indian. She lived to be one hundred and three years of age. Most of her life was spent in Texas as she went there to live when she was about fourteen years of age and never returned to the place of her birth. "I remember, says 'Aunt Lizzie,' that grandmother used to tell us that if we disobeyed her, she would come through the keyhole and 'witch' us. I really believed that grandma could come through the keyhole, so I stuffed it full of cotton." We were scared within an inch of our lives of grandpa because he would whip my uncles and I jes like Ol' Massa whipped the slaves, and then he used to tell us old, old slaves stories. One was bout John and Ned, slaves of Ol' Massa, way back there.

Ol' Massa had hundreds of beautiful hogs. Soon they began to disappear. He suspected John and Ned as they had absolute care of them. Then Ol' Massa's big blue barrow disappeared. He asked the boys about it but they "jes scratched their heads and acted worried too." When they would go to feed at night, Ned would sing: "Pig-o-wee. Pig-o-wee. Somebody's done been here and stole Massaa's big blue barrow. Pig-o-wee. Pig-o-wee. Somebody's done been here and stole Massa's big blue barrow. Pig-o-wee. Pig-o-wee."

One night Ol' Massa blacked up and waited for them. John came first and Ol' Massa locked him up and put on his clothes and waited for Ned. When Ned arrived he looked at Ol' Massa and said, "John is you sick, you sho looks bad?" "Bout dead," said Ol' Massa. They began their work of getting jes one more hog. Ned notices that John acted kinda funny. He didn't persuade that hog like he always did. Anyway they drove the hog down to the river where they had to cross to their hut. Ned looked at Ol' Massa's face where the charcoal had rubbed off in the heat and scramble of stealing his own hog. "John you sho' must have the leprosy. Them spots on your face done tole me what it is." "Bout dead, bout dead," said Ol' Massa.

While they were crossing the river on the little homemade ferry made by the boys, Ned began to feel kinda queer, something told him that John was really Ol' Massa. Finally he gained courage enough to ask, "say yo ain't Ol' Massa, are you?" Ol' Massa answered, "Indeed I am, and if you and John don't return every hog you have stolen, I am going to give you five hundred licks each." Ned instantly jumped into the river and was never seen again.

Two things that I learned early besides work, was dancin' and cussin.' Took it up from my uncles, I guess. Grandpa would have killed me if he had known that I was a dancin! I would get my clothes off and go to bed early, then I would slip around and get my best homespun dress and brass toe shoes that had been polished and set away until time to go to church. Then I would slip out with my uncles and meet my man down the road away's. We danced until mornin'[,] then walk home. I would walk on the brush and rocks so that my shoes would not be slick on the bottom when I got home. Grandpa would call me about four o'clock every morning. "Black-chile, black-chile, time to help yo mammy fry them flapjacks." "Gettin' my clothes on right now," I answered, when in reality I was takin' em off. Without a wink of sleep I would pick or hoe cotton until sundown that day.

When grandpa finally found out about me, I was dancin' for money. Later I did some specialty acts. One was dancin' with a tumbler of water on my head for twenty-five minutes. The other was called "Lovin' My Man." I would dance with hightop [shoes] on, and they would be unbuttoned. My partner would stoop to button them for me. I would get my pistol out of my shirtwaist and shoot him down, without loosing a step. I made fifty dollars a night and a percentage of the net proceeds. Somebody brought Grandpa in the dance hall one night to see me dance. I heard him a screamin' "I'll kill her!" but I just kept a dancin' and thinkin' all the while that if he did kill me, I would die happy. I sho' loved to dance. Many times I would go off of the floor and cry and cry, caus I was so happy. I jes ate it up, and do you know what the devil had me do one time? He made me put a glass of water on my head and try to show my six little children how I used to dance. The glass fell on the floor and broke, and I was jes so clumsy. Jes' the devils work anyway.

"Aunt Lizzie" was married the first time, at the age of fifteen years. Her husband was also a good dancer. "He worked as a contractor and I continued to dance, made mo' money than he did." He used to croon this "love melody" to his Lizzie:

> *Somebody's eyes are very dark—*
> *Somebody's eyes are blue.*
> *Somebody's eyes are very dark.*
> *Bring my lover back to me.*
>
> *Bring, Oh! bring him back to me.*
> *Bring my lover back to me.*
> *Bring, Oh! bring him back to me.*
> *My love is like a little dove,*
> *That flies roun' in the air.*
> *Oh! when she's with another man*
> *No more she thinks of me.*
>
> *I wish, I wish my heart was glad*
> *So he could feel it through and through.*
> *Somebody's eyes are very dark.*
> *Somebody's eyes are blue.*
>
> *Bring, Oh! bring my lover back to me*
> *Bring my lover back to me*
> *Bring, Oh! bring her back to me.*

Aunt Lizzie doesn't care for love songs and dance melodies any longer, for she has traded them off for "spirituals," and these she sings continuously.

> *Hold to his hand.*
> *Hold to his hand.*

Hold to his hand.
Hold to God's unchangeable hand.

Oh! brother, hold to his hand.
Hold to his hand.
God's unchangeable hands.
Oh! sister, hold to God's unchangeable hands.

🐝 🐝 🐝

I shall not be removed.
I shall not—I shall not
Shall not be removed.

Just like a tree planteth by the water
I shall not be removed.
I am on my way to glory
I shall not be removed.

Tell my lovin' mother
I shall not be removed
I shall not—I shall not
I shall not be removed.

🐝 🐝 🐝

I came to Jesus, as I was
Feeling worried wawn and sad.
Found in him a restin' place.
And he has made me glad.

Lie down, lie down, you worried one,
With you head on my breast.
I found in him a restin' place,
And he has made me glad.

Trouble of every kind
Thank God, we always find.
Little talk with Jesus make it right,
Little talk with Jesus make it right.

Aunt Lizzie is superstitious, and believes in fortunes, however, she does not believe all fortune tellers, stories. "Some are sent by the 'Good Lowd' to warn us," she says.

"If a black and white cat passes you, good luck will come your way, but you bettah start to prayin' if a solid black cat crosses your path, cause bad luck sure catch up wid you."

Carrying an axe through the house is bad luck also. On Christmas morning, don't let a lady come into your house before a man does. If a man doesn't come in first, have a boy come into the house and go into every room and be seated. Good luck will be with you throughout the year.

Bad luck comes to the person who takes up ashes out of his stove and throws them out after sundown.

If you should happen to put your dress on wrong side out, wear it until twelve o'clock sharp, then turn it right side out and make a wish. The wish will come true.

Aunt Lizzie has had three husbands, and they were all good husbands, "cept they all alike in one way." Every morning they would yell out to me. "Get up from that bed and cook my breakfast," jes like grandpa used to yell at me. But I thinks I don't want another man, cause my seven chilluns say I am too old to cook breakfast for another one.

"Good-bye, white chile. Come back and see Auntie. Maybe I can think better for you next time. Good-bye."

LIZZIE FARMER

"Cousin Lizzie!"

"What."

"I'se seventy years old."

And I say, "Whut's you telling me for." I ain't got nothing to do with your age!

I knowed I was one year older than she was and it sorta riled me for her to talk about it. I never would tell folks my age for I knowed white folks didn't want no old woman working for 'em and I just wouldn't tell 'em how old I really was. Dat was nine years ago and I guess I'm seventy five now. I can't work much now.

I was born four years before de War.—"The one what set the cullud folks free." We lived on a big plantation in Texas. Old Master's name was John Booker and he was good to us all. My mammy died just at de close of de War and de young mistress took me and kept me and I growed up with her chillun. I thought I was quality sure nuff and I never would go to school 'cause I couldn't go 'long to de same school with de white chillun. Young mistress taught me how to knit, spin, weave, crochet, sew and embroider. I couldn't recollect my age and young Mistress told me to say, "I'se born de second year of de War dat set the cullud folks free," and the only time she ever git mad at me was when I forget to say it jest as she told me to. She take hold of me and shook me. I recollects all it, all de time.

Young mistress' name was Elizabeth Booker NcNew. I'se named after her. She finally gave me to my aunt when I was a big girl and I never lived wid white folks any more. I never saw my pappy till I was grown.

In the cullud quarters, we cooked on a fireplace in big iron pots. Our bread was baked in iron skillets with lids and we would set the skillet on de fire and put coals of fire on de lid. Bread was mighty good cooked like dat. We made our own candles. We had a candle mold and we would put a string in the center of the mold and pour melted tallow in it and let it harden. We would make eight at one time. Quality folks had brass lamps.

When we went to cook our vegetables we would put a big piece of hog jowl in de pot. We'd put in a lot of snap beans and when dey was about half done we'd put in a mess of cabbage and when it was about half done we'd put in some squash and when it was about half done we'd put in some okra. Then when it was done we would take it out a layer at a time. Go 'way! It makes me hungry to talk about it.

When we cooked possum dat was a feast. We would skin him and dress him and put him on top de house and let him freeze for two days or nights. Then we'd boil him with red pepper, and take him out and put him in a pan and slice sweet 'taters and put round him and roast him. My, dat was good eating.

It was a long time after de War 'fore all de niggers knowed dey was really free. My grandpappy was Master Booker's overseer. He wouldn't have a white man over his niggers. I saw grandpappy whip one man with a long whip. Master Booker was good and wouldn't whip 'em less'n he had to. De niggers dassent leave de farm without a pass for fear of de Ku Kluxers and patrolers.

We would have dances and play parties and have sho' nuff good times. We had "ring plays." We'd all catch hands and march round, den we'd drop all hands 'cept our pardners and we'd swing round and sing:

> *"You steal my pardner, and I steal yours,*
> *Miss Mary Jane.*
> *My true lover's gone away,*
> *Miss Mary Jane!*
>
> *"Steal all round and don't slight none,*
> *Miss Mary Jane.*
> *He's lost out but I'se got one,*
> *Miss Mary Jane!"*

We always played at log rollin's an' cotton pickin's.

Sometimes we would have a wedding and my what a good time we'd have. Old Master's daughter, Miss Janie, got married and it took us more'n three weeks to get ready for it. De house was cleaned from top to bottom and us chillun had to run errands. Seemed like we was allers under foot, at least dat was what mammy said. I never will fergit all the good things they cooked up. Rows of pies and cakes, baked chicken and ham, my, it makes my mouth water jest thinking of it. After de wedding and de feast de white folks danced all night and us cullud folks ate all night.

When one of de cullud folks die we would allers hold a "wake." We would set up with de corpse and sing and pray and at midnight we'd all eat and den we'd sing and pray some more.

In de evening after work was done we'd sit round and de older folks would sing songs. One of de favorites was:

> *"Miss Ca'line gal,*
> *Yes Ma'am*
> *Did you see dem buzzards?*
> *Yes Ma'am,*
> *Did you see dem floppin,'*
> *How did ye' like 'em?*
> *Mighty well.*
>
> *"Miss Ca'line gal,*
> *Yes Ma'am,*
> *Did you see dem buzzards?*
> *Yes Ma'am,*
> *Did you see dem sailin'?*
> *Yes Ma'am.*
> *How did you like 'em?*
> *Mighty well.*

I've heered folks talk about conjures and hoodoo charms. I have a hoss shoe over de door dat will bring good luck. I sho' do believe certain things bring bad luck. I hate to hear a scrinch (screech) owl holler at night. Whenever a scrinch owl git in dat tree at night and start to holler I gits me a stick and I say, "Confound you, I'll make yet set up dar and say 'Umph huh,'" so I goes out and time I gits dar he is gone. If you tie a knot in de corner of de bed sheet he will leave, or turn your hat wrong side out too. Dey's all good and will make a scrinch owl leave every time.

I believes in dreams and visions too. I dreamed one night dat I had tall palings all 'round my house and I went out in de yard and dere was a big black hoss and I say, "How come you is in my yard? I'll jest put you out jest lak you got in." I opened de gate but he wouldn't go out and finally he run in de door and through the house and went towards de East. Right after dat my son died. I saw dat hoss again de other night. A black hoss allus means death. Seeing it de other night mean I'se gwineter die.

I know one time a woman named May Runnels wanted to go to church about a mile away and her old man wouldn't go with her. It made her mad and she say, "I'll be damned if I don't go." She had to go through a grave yard and when she was about half way across it a icy hand jest slap her and her mouth was twisted way 'round fer about three months. Dat was a lesson to her fer cussing.

One time there was a nigger what belonged on a adjoining farm to Master John Bookers and dey told us dis story:

"Dis nigger went down to de spring and found a terrapin and he say, 'What brung you here?' Jest imagine how he felt when it say to him, 'Teeth and tongue brung me here, and teeth and tongue will bring you here.' He run to de house and told his Master dat he found a terrapin dat could talk. Dey went back and he asked de terrapin what brung him here and it wouldn't say a word. Old Master didn't like it 'cause he went down there jest to see a common ordinary terrapin and he told de nigger he was going to git into trouble fer telling him a lie. Next day the nigger seen de terrapin and it say de same thing again. Soon after dat dis nigger was lynched right close to de place he saw de terrapin."

Master John Booker had two niggers what had a habit of slipping across de river and killing old Master's hogs and hiding de meat in de loft of de house. Master had a big blue hog and one day he missed him and he sent Ned to look fer him. Ned knowed all de time dat he had killed it and had it hid in his loft. He hunted and called "Pig-ooie, Pig." Somebody done stole old Master's big blue hog. Dey couldn't find it but old Master thought Ned knowed something 'bout it. One night he found out Ned was gonna kill another hog and had asked John to go with him. He borrowed John's clothes and blackened his face and met Ned at de river. Soon dey find a nice big one and Ned say, "John, I'll drive him round and you kill him." So he drove him past old Master but he didn't want to kill his own hog so he made lak he'd like to kill him but he missed him. Finally Ned got tired and said, "I'll kill him, you drive him by me." So Master John drove him by and Ned knock de hog on de head and cut his throat and dey load him on de canoe. When dey was nearly 'cross de river Old Master dip up some water and wash his face a little, then he look at Ned and he say, "Ned you look sick, I believe you've got lepersy." Ned row on little more and he jump in de river and Master had a hard time finding him again. He had the overseer whip Ned for that.

I think Lincoln was a wonderful man. Everybody was sorry when he died, but I never heerd of Jeff Davis.

Sonny Greer

❦ ❦ ❦

Age 88 Years
Red River County

I was born in Arkansas, January 6, 1850. My father was Henry Rogers Greer and mother was Lucena Greer. She was born in Mississippi and was sold several times.

The master was Hugh Rogers. He had four boys—Jim, who died just about the time war started, John, Hugh and Sam. The girls were Caroline, Easter, Mary, Annie, Susie.

My wife is named Phyllis. We were married at Clarksville, Red River County, Texas, on March 4, 1874. She was eighteen and belonged to the Wortham's during slave days. We had no children, but I had some brothers and sisters. There was Harry and Shedrick, and Violet, Betsy, America, Jane, Ann, Delsey and Delsey [*sic*]. They all stayed in Texas.

The master took his slaves, said there was 80 or 90, to Texas when the war got started. We was refugees. Down there we built one room log cabins for the slaves. They had no porches and the quarters was without furniture, just home made beds.

I worked in the fields raising cotton and tobacco. Start to work at daylight and quit when the sun went down. Then lots of nights work around the house. Plenty of work to do, but no money until after the war. Then I worked for the same master. He paid me fifty cents a day.

The master bought good heavy clothes for winter but in the summer we was about naked.

When a slave needed a whipping he got it. I was never whipped but lots of the negroes were. We had to have passes when going off the plantation. The patrollers would pick up the ones without a pass and they had the right to whip—just the same as if they was the master. I never saw any slave run away. But I heard about them.

Christmas time wasn't much different that [*sic*] any other, except if it come in the middle of the week we got the rest of the week to ourselves. Just take care of the light chores. If Christmas come on Saturday then we had to be ready for work on the next Monday.

The master told us about freedom on August 4, 1865. He called everybody to the big house. I stayed on and worked, like I said, for fifty cents a day.

We never learned to read or write. The master didn't think it was right for slaves to learn.

My mind is not so good anymore. It is hard to remember things. I can't think good. That's why I can't tell more about the slave days.

Mattie Hardman

❦ ❦ ❦

Age 78 Years

I was born January 2, 1859, at Gunalis [Gonzales?], Texas. My father's name was William Tensley and my mother's name Mildred Howard. They was brought from Virginia. I did have 8 brothers and sisters but all of them are dead.

My Master was name William Henry Howard. Since I was too young to work I nursed my sisters' children while they worked. The cooking was done all up to the general kitchen at Masters house and when slaves come from work they would send their children up to the kitchen to bring their meals to their homes in the quarters. Our Mistress would have one of the cooks to dish up vegetables and she herself would slice or serve the meat to see that it wasn't wasted, as seemingly it was thought so precious.

As my mother worked 'round the Big House quite a deal I would go up to the Big House with her and play with the white children who seemed to like for me to come to play with them. One day in anger while playing I called one of the white girls, "old black dog" and they pretended they would tell their mother (my mistress) about it. I was scared, as they saw, and they promised me they would not tell if I'd promise to not do it again, and which I was so glad to do and be let off so lightly.

For summer I wore a cotton slip and for winter my mother knitted at nights after her days work was done so I wore red flannels for underwear and thick linsey for an over-dress, and had knitted stockings and bought shoes. As my master was a doctor he made his slaves wear suitable clothes in accordance to the weather. We also wore gloves my mother knitted in winter.

My Mistress was good to all of the slaves. On Sunday morning she would make all the Negro children come to the Big House and she would stand on the front steps and read the Catechism to us who sat or stood in front on the ground.

My Master was also good. On Wednesdays and Friday nights he would make the slaves come up to the Big House and he would read the Bible to them and he would pray. He was a doctor and very fractious and exact. He didn't allow the slaves to claim they forgot to do thus and so nor did he allow them to make the expression, "I thought so and so." He would say to them if they did: "Who told you, you could think!"

They had 10 children, 7 boys and 3 girls. Their house was a large 2-story log house painted white. My father was overseer on the plantation.

The plantation consisted of 400 acres and about 40 slaves including children. The slaves were so seldom punished until they never'd worry about being punished. They treated their slaves as though they loved them. The poor white neighbors were also good and treated the slaves good, for my Master would warn them not to bother his Negroes. My Mistress always told the slaves she wanted all of them to visit her and come to her funeral and burial when she died and named the men slaves she wanted to be her pall-bearers, all of which was carried out as she planned even though it was after freedom.

The slaves even who lived adjoining our plantation would have church at our Big House. They would hold church on Sundays and Sunday nights.

As my mother worked a deal for her Mistress she had an inkling or overheard that they was going to be set free long before the day they were. She called all the slaves on the plantation together and broke to them this news after they had promised her they would not spread the news so that it would get back to our Master. So, everybody kept the news until Saturday night June 19th, when Master called all the slaves to the big gate and told them they were all free, but could stay right on in their homes if they had no places to go and which all of them did. They went right out and gathered the crop just like they'd always done, and some of them remained there several years.

My first husband was name, S. W. Warnley. We had 4 children, 1 girl and three boys and 3 grandchildren. I now have two grandchildren.

Now that slavery is over I sometime wish 'twas still existing for some of our lazy folks, so that so many of them wouldn't or couldn't loaf around so much lowering our race, walking streets day by day and running from house to house living corruptible lives which is keeping the race down as though there be no good ones among us.

George W. Harmon

🐝 🐝 🐝

Age 83 Years
Lamar County

I was born December 25, 1854, in Lamar County, Texas. I don't know my real age, but I was 9 years old at Freedom, June 14, 1863 [*sic*]. My father was named Charles Harmon and mother Mary Roland, after her owners. My father come from Tennessee and my mother from Virginia.

Well, my brother-in-law was named Daniel and the other one named John; my sisters were named Huldy and Polly. During slavery we had wood beds and mattresses were spun and woven for them. Some of the mattresses were stuffed with moss that had been buried to kill it so that it wouldn't grow.

The first and only money I earned was when I cleaned and shined a pair of boots for a white man and he gave me $5.00 of Confederate money. Don't remember what I did with it.

In hot weather we wore only shirts made of home made cotton and split up each side, and if they didn't have any cloth they would take a crocus sack and cut holes in each corner for arm holes and in the center for the head and wear that. In cold weather we wore woven cloth called drilling for underwear, and a kind of cloth called hickory check for shirts and made into cloth for trousers. On Saturdays the clothes were washed to have clean for Sunday. My father was a shoemaker and we wore the coarse brogans.

When I was married, my wedding clothes were good. I married Margaret Blunt of Lamar County, Texas. My Master, Mistress and their children were very good to their slaves. They lived in a log house, two stories high.

The overseer was one of the negro slaves who was more evil and meaner than our Master. My owner owned two plantations about 300 or 400 acres. He owned one family of negroes and my mother, totaling eight in number. The slaves were whipped for any misdemeanor dislikeable. One lady was charged with stealing some home-made twisted tobacco and her owner made her lie down and whipped her until she fainted, then turned her over and hit her in the face to see if that would bring her to.

I never saw a sale of any slaves but when Lincoln was talking of freeing the negroes an agent came around and appraised all of us and said that the Government was thinking of buying us free.

In slavery an old man was said to be a conjurer, who had all kinds of snakes and insects. He took sick and died and the saying is that after he had died one night he came back and carried his box of insects and snakes out of the house and set them down and nobody could even go and get his body as these insects and snakes would come up and run them away.

The church of that day was held under brush arbors and though they could not read they would preach of better times and conditions.

I always would fight even my Master's children, and one day I had a stick and was about to hit one of Master's boys when one negro child ran and told my Master. He sent for me and told me that if I ever hit one of his children he would skin me and feed my hide to his hounds and it seemed he said that those hounds were just waiting for him to feed them.

During slavery there was one slave who would not work only when he chose and when they would get at him to whip him, he was so fast a runner they could not catch him. He could run so fast that he named or called himself "Bird in the Air." So my Master learned of a white fellow who made a specialty of running and had the reputation of catching any slaves who might be uncatchable. So my Master sent for this fellow and had warned this fast-running slave that he had sent for this runner to catch him whose title or reputation was heard of as "Hawk-running-son-of-a-gun," to catch the slave, "Bird-in-the-Air."

So on the day he was to arrive, "Bird-in-the-Air" awaited his arrival. When he arrived he went into Masters house to receive orders of whom to catch and after getting all details he and Master came out and went to where this slave lived and just when they reached the cabin where "Bird-in-the-Air" was, he ran out and hollowed, "Bird-in-the-Air." This white slave-catcher replied to him, "Yes and the hawk is after you!"

So the chase begun and "Hawk-running-son-of-a-gun" caught him within a half an hour, and with power to hold him until Master and others on horses arrived who took him in charge and whipped him. From that day on all that was necessary in controlling "Bird-in-the-Air" was to warn him by saying, "If you don't do so-and-so I'll send again for 'Hawk-running-son-of-a-gun!'"

Lincoln was a durn fool man, but he was better'n John de Baptist; next to Christ. Don't think much of Jefferson Davis. He's durn poor trash. As to Booker T. Washington I like him better'n [Frederick] Douglas[s] 'cause Douglas[s] married [a] white woman.

Annie Hawkins

☙ ☙ ☙

Age 90 Years

I calls myself 90, but I don't know jest how old I really am but I was a good sized gal when we moved from Georgia to Texas. We come on a big boat and one night the stars fell. Talk about being scared! We all run and hid and hollered and prayed. We thought the end of the world had come.

I never had no whitefolks that was good to me. We all worked jest like dogs and had about half enough to eat and got whupped for everything. Our days was a constant misery to us. I know lots of niggers that was slaves had a good time but we never did. Seems hard that I can't say anything good for any of 'em but I sho' can't. When I was small my job was to tote cool water to the field to the hands. It kept me busy going back and forth and I had to be sho' my old Mistress had a cool drink when she wanted it, too. Mother and my sister and me worked in the field all day and come [home] in time to clear away the things and cook supper. When we was through in the kitchen we would spin fer a long time. Mother would spin and we would card.

My old Master was Dave Giles, the meanest man that ever lived. He didn't have many slaves, my mammy, and me, and my sister, Uncle Bill, and Truman. He had owned my grandma but he give her a bad whupping and she never did git over it and died. We all done as much work as a dozen niggers—we knowed we had to.

I seen old Master git mad at Truman and he buckled him down across a barrel and whupped him till he cut the blood out of him and then he rubbed salt and pepper in the raw places. It looked like Truman would die it hurt so bad. I know that don't sound reasonable that a white man in a Christian community would do such a thing but you can't realize how heartless he was. People didn't know about it and we dassent tell for we knowed he'd kill us if we did. You must remember he owned us body and soul and they wasn't anything we could do about it. Old Mistress and her three girls was mean to us too.

One time me and my sister was spinning and old Mistress went to the well-house and she found a chicken snake and killed it. She brought it back and she throwed it around my sister's neck. She jest laughed and laughed about it. She thought it was a big joke.

Old Master stayed drunk all the time. I reckon that is the reason he was so fetched mean. My, how we hated him! He finally killed hisself drinking and I remember Old Mistress called us in to look at him in his coffin. We all marched by him slow like and I jest happened to look up and caught my sister's eye and we both jest natchelly laughed—Why shouldn't we? We was glad he was dead. It's a good thing we had our laugh fer old Mistress took us out and whupped us with a broomstick. She didn't make us sorry though.

Old Master and Mistress lived in a nice big house on top of a hill and us darkies lived in log cabins with log floors. Our dresses was made out of coarse cloth like cotton sacking and it sho' lasted a long time. It ort to been called mule-hide for it was about that tough.

We went to church sometimes. They had to let us do that or folks would have found out how mean they was to us. Our Master'd give us a pass to show the patroller. We was glad to git the chance to git away and we always went to church.

During the War we seen lots of soldiers. Some of them was Yankees and some were Sesesh soldiers. My job every day was to take a big tray of food and set it on a stump about a quarter of a mile from our house. I done this twice a day and ever time I went back the dishes would be empty. I never did see nobody and didn't nobody tell me why I was to take the food up there but of course it was either for soldiers that was scouting 'round or it may been for some lowdown dirty bushwhacker, and again it might a been for some of old Master's folks scouting 'round to keep out of the army.

We was the happiest folks in the world when we knowed we was free. We couldn't realize it at first but how we did shout and cry for joy when we did realize it. We was afraid to leave the place at first for fear old Mistress would bring us back or the pateroller would git us. Old Mistress died soon after the War and we didn't care either. She didn't never do nothing to make us love her. We was jest as glad as when old Master died. I don't know what become of the three gals. They was about grown.

We moved away jest as far away as we could and I married soon after. My husband died and I married again. I been married four times and all my husbands died. The last time I married it was to a man that belonged to a Indian man, Sam Love. He was a good owner and was one of the best men that ever lived. My husband never did move far away from him and he loved him like a father. He always looked after him till he died. My husband has been dead five years.

I have had fifteen children. Four pairs of twins, and only four of them are living. The good Lawd wouldn't let me keep them. I'se lived through three wars so you see I'se no baby.

Annie Hawkins

Ida Henry

Age 83 Years
Harrison County

I was born in Marshall, Texas, in 1854. Me mother was named Millie Henderson and me father Silas Hall. Me mother was sold in South Carolina to Mister Hall, who brought her to Texas. Me father was born and raised by Master John Hall. Me mother's and father's family consisted of five girls and one boy. My sister's names were: Margrette, Chalette, Lottie, Gracy and Loyo, and me brother's name was Dock Howard. I lived with me mother and father in a log house on Master Hall's plantation. We would be sorry when dark, as de patrollers would walk through de quarters and homes of de slavers all times of night wid pine torch lights to whip de niggers found away from deir home.

At nights when me mother would slip away for a visit to some of de neighbors homes, she would raise up the old plank floor of de log cabin and make pallets on de ground and put us to bed and put the floor back down so dat we couldn't be seen or found by the patrollers on their stroll around at nights.

My grandmother Lottie would always tell us not to let Master catch you in a lie, and to always tell him de truth.

I was house girl to me Mistress and nursed, cooked, and carried de children to and from school. In summer we girls wore cotton slips and yarn dresses for winter. When I got married I was dress in blue serge and was de third person to marry in it. Wedding dresses was not worn after de wedding in dem days by niggers as we was taught by our Mistress dat it was bad luck to wear de wedding dress after marriage. Therefore, 'twas handed down from one generation to the other one.

Me Mistress was sometimes good and sometimes mean. One day de cook was waiting de table and when passing around de potatoes, old Mistress felt of one and as hit wasn't soft done, she exclaimed to de cook, "What you bring these raw potatoes out here for?" and grab a fork and stuck it in her eye and put hit out. She, de cook, lived about 10 years and died.

Me Mistress was de mother of five children, Crock, Jim, Boss and two girls name, Lea and Annie.

Dere home was a large two-story white house wid de large white posts.

As me Master went to de War de old overseer tried himself in meanness over de slaves as seemingly he tried to be important. One day de slaves caught him and one held him whilst another knocked him in de head and killed him.

Master's plantation was about 300 acres and he had 'bout 160 slaves. Before de slaves killed our overseer, he would work 'em night and day. De slaves was punished when dey didn't do as much work as de overseer wanted 'em to do.

He would lock 'em in jail some nights without food and kept 'em dere all night, and after whipping 'em de next morning would only give 'em bread and water to work on till noon.

When a slave was hard to catch for punishment dey would make 'em wear ball and chains. De ball was 'bout de size of de head and made of lead.

On Sunday mornings before breakfast our Mistress would call us together, read de Bible and show us pictures of de Devil in de Bible and tell us dat if we was not good and if we would steal and tell lies dat old Satan would git us.

Close to our Master's plantation lived several families of old "poor white trash" who would steal me Master's hogs and chickens and come and tell me Mistress dat dey seen some of de slaves knock one of dere hogs in de head. Dis continued up till Master returned from de War and caught de old white trash stealing his hogs. De niggers did at times steal Master's hogs and chickens, and I would put biscuits and pieces of chicken in a sack under me dress dat hung from me waist, as I waited de table for me Mistress, and later would slip off and eat it as dey never gave de slaves none of dis sort of food.

We had church Sundays and our preacher Rev. Pat Williams would preach and our Master and family and other nearby white neighbors would ofttime attend our services. De patrollers wouldn't allow de slaves to hold night services, and one night dey caught me mother out praying. Dey stripped her naked and tied her hands together and wid a rope tied to de hand cuffs and threw one end of de rope over a limb and tied de other end to de pommel of a saddle on a horse. As me mother weighed 'bout 200, dey pulled her up so dat her toes could barely touch de ground and whipped her. Dat same night she ran away and stayed over a day and returned.

During de fall months dey would have corn shucking and cotton pickings and would give a prize to de one who would pick de highest amount of cotton or shuck de largest pile of corn. De prize would usually be a suit of clothes or something to wear and which would be given at some later date.

We could only have dances during holidays, but dances was held on other plantations. One night a traveler visiting me Master wanted his boots shined. So Master gave de boots to one of de slaves to shine and de slave put de boots on and went to a dance and danced so much dat his feet swelled so dat when he returned he could not pull 'em off.

De next morning as de slave did not show up with de boots dey went to look for him and found him lying down trying to pull de boots off. He told his Master dat he had put de boots on to shine 'em and could not pull 'em off. So master had to go to town and buy de traveler another pair of boots. Before he could run away de slave was beaten wid 500 lashes.

De War dat brought our freedom lasted about two years. Me Master went and carried one of de slaves for a servant. When he returned he seemed a much different man dan he was before de War. He was kind and good and from dat day on he never whipped another slave nor did he allow any of his slaves whipped. Dis time lasted from January to June de 19th when we was set free in de State of Texas.

Lincoln and Davis both died short of promise. I means dat dey both died before dey carried out dere plans and promises for freeing de slaves.

Lewis Jenkins

❦ ❦ ❦

Age 93 Years

I was born in Green County, Alabama in January 1844.

My mother was a white woman and her name was Jane Jenkins. My father was a nigger. He was a coachman on my Master's place. I was told this in 1880 by the white doctor, Lyth Smith, which brung me into the world. My Master, who was my grandfather, brung me to Texas when I was jest 7 or 8 years old. A few years later, he brung my mother down to Texas and she had with her three boys, which was her children and my brothers. They was white children and name Jones. They first names was Tom, Joe and Lije. They parted from me and I never heered no more about 'em. I didn't even know my mother when I seen her. All my life I done jest knowed my white kinfolks and nothing 'tall about the other part of my color.

Before I was born, my mother was tucken away from her playmates and kept in the attic hid. They tuck me soon as I was born from her. When her time to be in bed was up, she'd ask the waitman whar I was at. The waitman was Dr. Lyth Smith. He'd tell her I was at Ann's house. I never got a chance to nurse my mother. After she got up and come down, she wanted to see her baby. Now she goes to Ann's house and couldn't find me. After she couldn't find me there, she looked in all the houses on the place for me, her baby. Then she commenced screaming, tearing her clothes off and tearing her hair out. They sent her to the calaboose till they could git her some clothes to put on. She went distracted. She tore out towards town. The way they got her to hush, they tole her I was with my grandma. They had me hid on the road to Texas. The doctor's wife said I was the first nigger she shed a tear over. It was a destruction thing. Well, that scandalized the family and they moved to Texas, and come by and got me and tuck me to Texas. When they crossed the big river, Tom Bigby [Tombigbee] River in Alabama, 3 miles wide on boat, the woman that had me in hand, was just churning me up and down in the river. They hollered at her, and I says that there's whar God tuck me in his bosom.

When I was 7 or 8 years old, the white folks tuck me in charge. They was gonna make me a watchman to watch for 'em at night. But when they begun this, I wasn't old enough to remember.

The first house I was sont to, was the cook's house. The cook said, "what you come down heah for?" I told her I didn't know. "Who sont you?" I said, "Old Master Jenkins." She knowed 'mediately what I was sont for, don't you see? She says to me, "Set down little rascal[;] I'll knock you in the head." Well, what could I do but set, child lak. Before long I was asleep and they tuck me out door. Next mawning I was told to go to the big house. Old Master axe "What'd you see last night?" I told him I didn't seed nothing. Now they got the cow hide an' hit me three or four licks and axe me 'at same question agin. I tole 'em I didn't seed nothing. This went on for 'bout a hour. I had to take a whipping ever mawning, 'cause I had to go to ever house and never seen nothing. The last house I went to, well, in the mawning as I was gwine back to the big house, a voice come to me and said, "See nothing, tell nothing." It meant for me not to lie and on and on as I growed for years to come, as I was big enough to plow corn, I was out in the field and a voice, that same voice too, said, "Iffen I was you, I'd leave this place, 'cause you'll come to want and won't have." All this was the causing of my conversion.

My first job was scouring floors and I mean I scoured 'em too. Next I scoured knives and forks. From 'at job I went into real work, and no play.

My master and his family jest lived in a log house. My mistress was my grandfather's wife and my grandmother, but I couldn't claim her. Her and her oldest child treated me some rough. I never had no good time till that old white woman died, and talking about somebody glad she died, I sure was. They tuck turns about treating me bad.

There was about 20 slaves on our place, children and all. Dewan, which was my uncle, was the overseer. He waked us up jest before sunrise and we worked from sun to sun. I seen 'em tie niggers hand and foot to mill posts and whip 'em with bull whips. Them was neighbors' though, not our'n. They whipped the women by pulling they dresses down to they hips and beat 'em till they was satisfied. For myself, my grandfather whipped me till his dog tuck pity on me and tried to drag me away. This is the scar on my leg whar he pulled on me. He was beating me till I said, "Oh! Pray Master." He didn't tell me till after he was through beating me though.

I seen 'em sell people, what wasn't able to work from the block jest lak cattle. They would be chained togedder. They tuck mothers from children even just a week old and sell 'em. They stripped the slaves, women and all and let the bidders look at 'em to see iffen they was scarred before they would buy 'em.

Them old white folks wouldn't learn us to read and write and wouldn't let they youngins learn us. My youngest mistress, which was my auntie 'mind you, was trying to learn me to read and write and was caught and she got some whipping, almost a killing.

I never seen but one nigger man hung. He was crippled and had run away. I seen dis wid my own eyes, no guess work. He had caught a little white girl, school girl, too, ravaged her and cut off her tongue off. Oh, that was barbous. He oughta been burnt. He didn't git his jest due at hanging.

Patterollers was sure through the country. They was out to keep down nigger and white mixing and to keep niggers from having liberty to go out 'specially at night. They didn't 'low you to come to see a gall 'less she was 18 and you was 21. The cause of this was to raise good stock. The gals couldn't marry till they was 18 neither, but dey could have children. You had to have a pass to go see your gal even. Now you got your pass from your master. Iffen you was under 15, you could go play and didn't need no pass, but all over 15 jest had to have a pass.

They would go right to bed after they et. No Saturday off, jest washday. Some Sundays old mistress let us have sugar, flour and lard.

We was in a great game country and sure et our fill of coons, 'possums, rabbits, deer, turkeys and the sich and things people wouldn't notice now. Cornbread and sweet potatoes was my fav-*rite* foods. Milk and butter was best eating.

We jest wore what you call slips wid jest two sleeves slipped over our head. No buttons. We wore the same thing in winter, jest heavier. Never wore no shoes till I was old enough to chop cotton.

At weddings they wore stripes all the time. They made 'em on hand looms. They was mostly white and red stripes.

We played marbles and ring plays. We used to sing this ditty during playing:

> *So many pretty gals*
> *So they say*
> *So many pretty gals*
> *So they say.*
> *Jest peep through the window Susie gal.*

They used to scare me death talking 'bout ole raw head and bloody bones out in the yard. For me, that meant staying in a mighty long time and having a fit to boot.

We used onions to keep off consumption. They was a family taken the black disease and they all died but one and he was ready to die. They tuck him out to burn the house up to keep that disease from spreading. They put the nigger in a house full of onions and he got sure enough well. The doctor said the onions had cured him. We sure believed in our onions and do till today. Even the next mawning after he was put in the house and couldn't walk[,] he axe for some milk.

That war that freed the niggers started in 1861. I had two young Masters to go. It lasted 4 years. They was figuring on taking me that very next year, and it was so fixed that the war ended. We had a big drought during the war, which made it bad on the soldiers. I never seen the Yankees only when they was passing 'long the road. One day whilst we was eating our dinner, our Master said, "All you, young and old, when you git through come out on the gallery, I got something to tell you." When we got through we all trooped out and he said, "This is military law, but I am forced to tell you." He says, "This law says free the nigger, so now you is jest as free as me by this law. I can't make you all stay wid me 'less you want to, therefore you can go any place you want to." That was about laying-by crop time in June. It was on June 19th an' we still celebrates 'at day in Texas, 'at is "Nigger Day" down there. He say, "I'd lak for you to stay till the crops is laid by iffen you will.["] Iffen it hadn't been for his wife maybe we would've stayed on, but she jest kept bossing the nigger women and we jest didn't lak it and that's what brung on the scatter. I left my old Master and went wid one of my young Masters, which was my uncle.

I was sure once tickled at my young Master. I done broke in a mule for him and he got on him one night and go jine the Ku Klux band. He had to go 'bout 4 miles. He got jest 'bout one mile and they come to two trees with a real white stone in 'twixt the trees. The mule seen this and throwed my Master off and hurt him something terrible. He come back and told his wife what done happened. He said, "Damn the Ku Klux." He never went to jine 'em no more.

I never went to school in my life. Never had the opportunity, 'cause I never had no kinfolks to own me or give me advice or help me. White kinfolks jest bossed me. I was jest lak a orphan. White folks will mess you up and be so treacherous.

I married Jane Deckers. The white man jest read out of the Bible and put our names and ages in the Bible and 'at was all the ceremony we had. I got three children and four grandchildren. One do stone work, another brick work and my daughter, housework.

I think Abe Lincoln was next to Jesus Christ. The best human man ever lived. He died helping the poor nigger man. Old Jeff Davis was right in his place. He was trying to help his race. He wasn't nothing lak right. It was God's plan that ever man be free. I don't believe Davis believed in right.

I am sure glad slavery is over. I glory in it. I trust and pray it'll never be again.

I think the church is the gospel way and ever body ought to be on it. The Baptist is my dear belief, 'cause I was baptized by the spirit and they by the water, nothing but the Baptist. I belongs to the Shiloh Baptist Church, right here on the West Side.

Mary Lindsay

❦ ❦ ❦

Age 91 Years
Fannin County

My slavery days wasn't like most people tell you about, 'cause I was give to my young Mistress and sent away to Texas when I was jest a little girl, and I didn't live on a big plantation a very long time.

I got an old family Bible what say I was born on September 20, in 1846, but I don't know who put de writing in it unless it was my mammy's mistress. My mammy had de book when she die.

My mammy come out to the Indian country from Mississippi two years before I was born. She was the slave of a Chickasaw part-breed name Sobe Love. He was the kinsfolks of Mr. Benjamin Love, and Mr. Henry Love what bring two big bunches of the Chickasaws out from Mississippi to the Choctaw country when the Chickasaws sign up de treaty to leave Mississippi, and the whole Love family settle 'round on the Red River below Fort Washita. There whar I was born.

My mammy say dey have a terrible hard time again the sickness when they first come out into that country, because it was low and swampy and all full of cane brakes, and everybody have the smallpox and the malaria and fever all the time. Lots of the Chickasaw families nearly died off.

Old Sobe Love marry her off to a slave named William, what belong to a full-blood Chickasaw man name Chick-a-lathe, and I was one of de children.

De children belong to the owner of the mother, and me and my brother Franklin, what we called "Bruner," was born under the name of Love and then old Master Sobe bought my pappy William, and we was all Love slaves then. My mammy had two more girls, name Hetty and Rena.

My mammy name was Mary, and I was named after her. Old Mistress name was Lottie, and they had a daughter name Mary. Old Master Sobe was powerful rich, and he had about a hundred slaves and four or five big pieces of that bottom land broke out for farms. He had niggers all on the places, but he didn't have no overseers, jest hisself and he went around and seen that everybody behave and do they work right.

Old Master Sobe was a mighty big man in the tribe, and so was all his kinfolks, and they went to Fort Washita and to Boggy Depot all the time on business, and leave the Negroes to look after old Mistress and the young daughter. She was almost grown along about that time, when I can first remember about things.

'Cause my name was Mary, and so was my mammy's and my young Mistress' too. Old Master Sobe called me Mary-Ka-Chubbe to show which Mary he was talking about.

Miss Mary have a black woman name Vici what wait on her all the time, and do the carding and spinning and cooking 'round the house, and Vici belong to Miss Mary. I never did go 'round the Big House, but jest stayed in the quarters with my mammy and pappy and helped in the field a little.

Then one day Miss Mary run off with a man and married him, and old Master Sobe nearly went crazy! The man was name Bill Merrick, and he was a poor blacksmith and didn't have two pair of britches to his name, and old Master Sobe said he jest stole Miss Mary 'cause she was rich, and no other reason. 'Cause he was a white man and she was mostly Chickasaw Indian.

Anyways old Master Sobe wouldn't even speak to Mr. Bill, and wouldn't let him set foot on the place. He jest reared and pitched around, and threatened to shoot him if he set eyes on him, and Mr. Bill took Miss Mary and left out for Texas. He set up a blacksmith shop on the big road between Bonham and Honey Grove, and lived there until he died.

Miss Mary done took Vici along with her, and pretty soon she come back home and stay a while, and old Master Sobe kind of soften up a little bit and give her some money to git started on, and he give her me too.

Dat jest nearly broke my old mammy's and pappy's heart, to have me took away off from them, but they couldn't say nothing and I had to go along with Miss Mary back to Texas. When we git away from the Big House I jest cried and cried until I couldn't hardly see, my eyes was so swole up, but Miss Mary said she gwine to be good to me.

I ask her how come Master Sobe didn't give her some of the grown boys and she say she reckon it because he didn't want to help her husband out none, but jest wanted to help her. If he give her a man her husband have him working in the blacksmith shop, she reckon.

Master Bill Merrick was a hard worker, and he was more sober than most the men in them days, and he never tell me to do nothing. He jest let Miss Mary tell me what to do. They have a log house close to the shop, and a little patch of a field at first, but after awhile he git more land, and then Miss Mary tell me and Vici we got to help in the field too.

That sho' was hard living then! I have to git up at three o'clock sometimes so I have time to water the hosses and slop the hogs and feed the chickens and milk the cows, and then git back to the house and git the breakfast. That was during the times when Miss Mary was having and nursing her two children, and old Vici had to stay with her all the time. Master Bill never did do none of that kind of work, but he had to be in the shop sometimes until way late in the night, and sometimes before daylight, to shoe peoples hosses and oxen and fix wagons.

He never did tell me to do that work, but he never done it his own self and I had to do it if anybody do it.

He was the slowest one white man I ever did see. He jest move 'round like de dead lice falling off'n him all the time, and everytime he go to say anything he talk so slow that when he say one word you could walk from here to way over there before he say de next word. He don't look sick, and he was powerful strong in his arms, but he acts like he don't feel good jest the same.

I remember when the War come. Mostly by the people passing 'long the big road, we heard about it. First they was a lot of wagons hauling farm stuff into town to sell, and then purty soon they was soldiers on the wagons, and they was coming out into the country to git the stuff and buying it right at the place they find it.

Then purty soon they commence to be little bunches of mens in soldier clothes riding up and down the road going somewhar. They seem like they was mostly young boys like, and they jest laughing and jollying and going on like they was on a picnic.

Then the soldiers come 'round and got a lot of the white men and took them off to the War even iffen they didn't want to go. Master Bill never did want to go, 'cause he had his wife and two little children, and anyways he was gitting all the work he could do fixing wagons and shoeing hosses, with all the traffic on de road at that time. Master Bill had jest two hosses, for him and his wife to ride and to work to the buggy, and he had one old yoke of oxen and some more cattle. He got some kind of paper in town and he kept it with him all the time, and when the soldiers would come to git his hosses or his cattle he would jest draw that paper on 'em and they let 'em alone.

By and by the people got so thick on the big road that they was somebody in sight all the time. They jest keep a dust kicked up all day and all night 'cepting when it rain, and they git all bogged down and be strung all up and down the road camping. They kept Master Bill in the shop all the time, fixing the things they bust trying to git the wagons out'n the mud. They was whole families of them with they children and they slaves along, and they was coming in from every place because the Yankees was gitting in their part of the country, they say.

We all git mighty scared about the Yankees coming but I don't reckon they ever git thar, 'cause I never seen none, and we was right on the big road and we would of seen them. They was a whole lot more soldiers in them brown looking jeans, round-about jackets and cotton britches a-faunching up and down the road on their hosses, though. Them hoss soldiers would come b'iling by, going east, all day and night, and then two-three days later on they would all come tearing by going west! Dey acted like dey didn't know whar dey gwine, but reckon dey did.

Den Master Bill git sick. I reckon he more wore out and worried than anything else, but he go down with de fever one day and it raining so hard Mistress and me and Vici can't neither one go nowhar to git no help.

We puts peach tree poultices on his head and wash him off all the time, until it quit raining so Mistress can go out on de road, and then a doctor man come from one of the bunches of soldiers and see Master Bill. He say he going be all right and jest keep him quiet, and go on.

Mistress have to tend de children and Vici have to take care of Master Bill and look after the house, and dat leave me all by myself wid all the rest of everything around the place.

I got to feed all the stock and milk the cows and work in the field too. Dat the first time I ever try to plow, and I nearly git killed, too! I got me a young yoke of oxens I broke to pull the wagon, 'cause Vici have to use the old oxens to work the field. I had to take the wagon and go 'bout ten miles west to a patch of woods Master Bill owned to git fire wood, 'cause we

lived right on a flat patch of prairie, and I had to chop and haul the wood by myself. I had to git postoak to burn in the kitchen fireplace and willow for Master Bill to make charcoal out of to burn in his blacksmith fire.

Well, I hitch up them young oxen to the plow and they won't follow the row, and so I go git the old oxens. One of them old oxens didn't know me and took in after me, and I couldn't hitch 'em up. And then it begins to rain again.

After the rain was quit I git the bucket and go milk the cows, and it is time to water the hosses too, so I starts to the house with the milk and leading one of the hosses. When I gits to the gate I drops the halter across my arm and hooks the bucket of milk on my arm too, and starts to open the gate. The wind blow the gate wide open, and it slap the hoss on the flank. That was when I nearly git killed!

Out the hoss go through the gate to the yard, and down the big road, and my arm all tangled up in the halter rope and me dragging on the ground!

The first jump knock the wind out of me and I can't git loose, and that hoss drag me down the road on the run until he meet up with a passel of soldiers and they stop him.

The next thing I knowed I was laying on the back kitchen gallery, and some soldiers was pouring water on me with a bucket. My arm was broke, and I was stove up so bad that I have to lay down for a whole week, and Mistress and Vici have to do all the work.

Jest as I getting able to walk 'round here come some soldiers and say they come to git Master Bill for the War. He still in the bed sick, and so they leave a parole paper for him to stay until he git well, and then he got to go into Bonham and go with the soldiers to blacksmith for them that got the cannons, the man said.

Mistress take on and cry and hold onto the man's coat and beg, but it don't do no good. She say they don't belong to Texas but they belong in the Chickasaw Nation, but he say that don't do no good, 'cause they living in Texas now.

Master Bill jest stew and fret so, one night he fever git way up and he go off into a kind of a sleep and about morning he died.

My broke arm begin to swell up and hurt me, and I git sick with it again, and Mistress git another doctor to come look at it.

He say I got bad blood from it how come I git so sick, and he git out his knife out'n his satchel and bleed me in the other arm. The next day he come back and bleed me again two times, and the next day one more time, and then I git so sick I puke and he quit bleeding me.

While I still sick Mistress pick up and go off to the Territory to her pappy and leave the children thar for Vici and me to look after. After while she come home for a day or two and go off again somewhere else. Then the next time she come home she say they been having big battles in the Territory and her pappy moved all his stuff down on the river, and she home to stay now.

We git along the best we can for a whole winter, but we nearly starve to death, and then the next spring when we getting a little patch planted Mistress go into Bonham and come back and say we all free and the War over.

She say, "You and Vici jest as free as I am, and a lot freer, I reckon, and they say I got to pay you if you work for me, but I ain't got no money to pay you. If you stay on with me and help me I will feed and home you and I can weave you some good dresses if you card and spin the cotton and wool."

Well, I stayed on, 'cause I didn't have no place to go, and I carded and spinned the cotton and wool and she make me just one dress. Vici didn't do nothing but jest wait on the children and Mistress.

Mistress go off again about a week, and when she come back I see she got some money, but she didn't give us any of it.

After a while I asked her ain't she got some money for me, and she say no, ain't she giving me a good home? Den I starts to feeling like I aint treated right.

Every evening I git done with the work and go out in the back yard and jest stand and look off to the west towards Bonham, and wish I was at that place or some other place.

Den along come a nigger boy and say he working for a family in Bonham and he git a dollar every week. He say Mistress got some kin-folks in Bonham and some of Master Sobe Love's niggers living close to there.

So one night I jest put that new dress in a bundle and set foot right down the big road a-walking west, and don't say nothing to nobody!

Its ten miles into Bonham, and I gits in town about daylight. I keeps on being afraid, 'cause I can't git it out'n my mind I still belong to Mistress.

Purty soon some niggers tells me a nigger name Bruner Love living down west of Greenville, and I know that my brother Franklin, 'cause we all called him Bruner. I don't remember how all I gits down to Greenville, but I know I walks most the way, and I finds Bruner. Him and his wife working on a farm, and they say my sister Hetty and my sister Rena what was little is living with my mammy way back up on the Red River. My pappy done died in time of the War and I didn't know it.

Bruner taken me in a wagon and we went to my mammy, and I lived with her until she died and Hetty married. Then I married a boy name

Henry Lindsay. His people was from Georgia, and he live with them way west at Cedar Mills, Texas. That was right close to Gordonville, on the Red River.

We live at Cedar Mills until three of my children was born and then we come to the Creek Nation in 1887. The last one was born here.

My oldest is named Georgia on account of her pappy. He was born in Georgia and that was in 1838, so his whitefolks got a book that say. My next child was Henry. We called him William Henry, after my pappy and his pappy. Then come Donie, and after we come here we had Madison, my youngest boy.

I lives with Henry here on this little place we got in Tulsa.

When we first come here we got some land for $15 an acre from the Creek Nation, but our papers said we can only stay as long as it is the Creek Nation. Then in 1901 comes the allotments, and we found out our land belong to a Creek Indian, and we have to pay him to let us stay on it. After while he makes us move off and we lose out all around.

But my daughter Donie git a little lot, and we trade it for this place about thirty year ago, when this town was a little place.

Bert Luster

☕ ☕ ☕

Age 85 Years

I'll be jest frank, I'm not for sho' when I was born, but it was in 1853. Don't know the month, but I was sho' born in 1853 in Watson County, Tennessee. You see my father was owned by Master Luster and my mother was owned by Masters Joe and Bill Asterns (father and son). I can remember when Master Astern moved from Watson County, Tennessee he brought me and my mother with him to Barnum County Seat [?], Texas. Master Astern owned about twelve slaves, and dey was all Astern 'cept Miriah Elmore's son Jim. He owned 'bout five or six hundred acres of ground, and de slaves raised and shucked all de corn and picked all de cotton. De whites folks lived in a big double log house and we slaves lived in log cabins. Our white folks fed us darkies! We ate nearly ever'thing dey ate. Dey ate turkey, chickens, ducks, geese, fish and we killed beef, pork, rabbits and deer. Yes, and possums too. And whenever we killed beef we tanned the hide and dere was a white man who made shoes for de white folks and us darkies. I tell you I'm not gonna lie, dem white folks was good to us darkies. We didn't have no mean overseer. Master Astern and his son jest told us niggers what to do and we did it, but 50 miles away dem niggers had a mean overseer, and dey called him "poor white trash," "old whooser," and sometime "old red neck," and he would sho' beat 'em turrible iffen dey didn't do jest like he wanted 'em to.

Seem like I can hear dem "nigger hounds" barking now. You see whenever a darky would get a permit to go off and wouldn't come back dey would put de "nigger hounds" on his trail and run dat nigger down.

De white women wove and spin our clothes. You know dey had looms, spins, and weavers. Us darkies would stay up all night sometime sep'rating cotton from the seed. When dem old darkies got sleepy dey would prop their eyes open wid straws.

Sho' we wore very fine clothes for dem days. You know dey dyed the cloth with poke berries.

We cradled de wheat on pins, caught the grain, carried it to de mill and had it ground. Sho,' I ate biscuits and cornbread too. Keep telling you dat we ate.

We got de very best care when we got sick. Don't you let nobody tell you dem white folks tried to kill out dem darkies 'cause when a darkey took sick dey would send and git de very best doctors round dat country. Dey would give us ice water when we got sick. You see we put up ice in saw dust in winter and when a slave got sick dey give him ice water, sometimes sage tea and chicken gruel. Dey wanted to keep dem darkies fat so dey could get top price for 'em. I never saw a slave sold, but my half brother's white folks let him work and buy hisself.

I was about 14, and I milked the cows, packed water, seeded cotton, churned milk up at de Big House and jest first one chore and den another. My mother cooked up at de Big House.

Dey was a lot of talk 'bout conjure but I didn't believe in it. Course dem darkies could do everything to one another, and have one another scared, but dey couldn't conjure dat overseer and stop him from beating 'em near to death. Course he didn't flog 'em till dey done sumping.

I married my woman, Nannie Wilkerson, 58 years ago. Dat was after slavery, and I love her, honest to God I does. Course in dem days we didn't buy no license, we jest got permits from old Master and jumped over a broom stick and jest got married.

I sho' did hate when the Yanks come 'cause our white folks was good to us, and jest take us right along to church with 'em. We didn't work on Sad'days or Christmas.

We raised gardens, truck patches and such for spending change.

I sho' caught hell after dem Yanks come. Befo' de war, you see de patroller rode all nite but wouldn't bother a darkey iffen he wouldn't run off. Why dem darkeys would run off I jest couldn't see.

Dose Yanks treated old master and mistress so mean. Dey took all his hams, chickens, and drove his cattle out of the pasture, but didn't bother us niggers honest. Dey drove old master Aster[n] off'n his own plantation and we all hid in de corn field.

My mother took me to Greenville, Texas, 'cause my step-pappy was one of dem half smart niggers round dere trying to preach and de Ku Klux Klan beat him half to death.

Dere was some white folks who would take us to church wid 'em—dis was aftah the war now—and one night we was all sitting up thar and one old woman with one leg was dah and when them Klans shot in amongst us niggers and white folks aunt Mandy beat all of us home. Yes suh.

My first two teachers was two white men, and dem Klans shot in de hotel what dey lived in, but dey had school for us niggers jest de same. After dat, dose Klans got so bad Uncle Sam sent soljers down dere to keep peace.

After de soljers come and run de Klans out we worked hard dat fall and made good crops. 'Bout three years later I came to Indian Territory in search of educating my kids.

I landed here 46 years ago on a farm not far from now Oklahoma City. I got to be a prosperous farmer. My bale of cotton amongst 5,000 bales won the blue ribbon at Guthrie, Oklahoma, and dat bale of cotton and being a good democrat won for me a good job as a clerk on the Agriculture Board at the State Capitol. All de white folks liked me and still like me and called me "cotton king."

I have jest three chillun living. Walter is parcel post clerk here at de post office downtown. Delia Jenkins, my daughter is a housewife and Cleo Luckett, my other daughter, a common laborer.

Have been a christian 20 years. Jest got sorry for my wicked ways. I am a member of the Church of God. My wife is a member of the Church of Christ. I'm a good democrat and she is a good republican.

My fav'rite song is: "Dark Was the Nite, and Cold the Ground" and "Couldn't Hear Nobody Pray."

I'm glad slavery is over, but I don't think dem white folks was fighting to free us niggers. God freed us. Of course, Abraham Lincoln was a pretty fine man. Don't know much about Jeff Davis. Never seen him. Yes, and Booker T. Washington. He was one of the Negro leaders. The first Negro to represent the Negroes in Washington. He was a great leader.

During slavery time never heerd of a cullud man commiting 'sault on a white woman. The white and cullud all went to church together too. Niggers and white shouted alike.

I remember some of the little games we played now: "Fox in the wall," "Mollie, Mollie Bride," and "Hide and go seek."

Allen V. Manning

❦ ❦ ❦

Age 87 Years
Coryell County

I always been somewhar in the South, mostly in Texas when I was a young man, and of course us Negroes never got much of a show in court matters, but I reckon if I had of had the chance to set on a jury I would of made a mighty poor out at it.

No sir, I jest can't set in judgement on nobody, 'cause I learned when I was jest a little boy that good people and bad people—makes no difference which—jest keep on living and doing like they been taught, and I jest can't seem to blame them none for what they do iffen they been taught that way.

I was born in slavery, and I belonged to a Baptist preacher. Until I was fifteen years old I was taught that I was his own chattel-property, and he could do with me like he wanted to, but he had been taught that way too, and we both believed it. I never did hold nothing against him for being hard on Negroes sometimes, and I don't think I ever would of had any trouble even if I had of growed up and died in slavery.

The young Negroes don't know nothing 'bout that today, and lots of them are rising up and amounting to something, and all us Negroes is proud of them. You see, it's because they been taught that they got as good a show to be something as anybody, if they tries hard.

Well, this old Negro knows one thing; they getting somewheres 'cause the young whitefolks is letting them and helping them to do it, 'cause the whitefolks has been taught the same way, and I praise God its getting to be that way, too. But it all go to show, people do like they been taught to do.

Like I say, my master was a preacher and a kind man, but he treated the Negroes jest like they treated him. He been taught that they was jest like his work hosses, and if they act like they his work hosses they git along all right. But if they don't—Oh, oh!

Like the Dixie song, I was born "on a frosty mornin" at the plantation in Clarke County, Mississippi, in the fall of 1850 they tell me. The old place looked the same all the time I was a child, clean up to when we pull out and leave the second year of the War.

I can shet my eyes and think about it and it seem to come right up in front of me jest like it looked. From my Pappy's cabin the Big House was off to the west, close to the big road, and most of the fields stretched off to the north. They was a big patch of woods off to the east, and no[t] much open land between us and the Chickasawhay River. Off to the southwest a few miles was the Bucatunna Creek, and the plantation was kind of in the forks between them, a little ways east of Quitman, Mississippi.

Old Master's people been living at that place a mighty long time, and most the houses and barns was old and been repaired time and time again, but it was a mighty pretty place. The Big House was built long, with a lot of rooms all in a row and a long porch, but it wasn't fine like a lot of the houses we seen as we passed by when we left that place to go to Louisiana.

Old Master didn't have any overseer hired, but him and his boys looked after the place and had a Negro called the driver. We-all shore hated that old black man, but I forget his name now. That driver never was allowed to think up nothing for the slaves to do, but jest was told to make them work hard at what the master and his boys told them to do. Whitefolks had to set them at a job and then old driver would whoopity and whoopity around, and egg them and egg them until they finish up, so they can go at something else. He worked hard hisself, though, and set a mighty hard pattern for the rest to keep up with. Like I say, he been taught he didn't know how to think, so he didn't try.

Old Mistress name was Mary, and they had two daughters, Levia and Betty. Then they had three sons. The oldest was named Bill Junior, and he was plumb grown when I was a boy, but the other two, Jedson and Jim, was jest a little older then me.

Old Master didn't have but two or three single Negroes, but he had several families, and most of them was big ones. My own family was pretty good size, but three of the children was born free. Pappy's name was William and Mammy's was Lucy. My brother Joe was the oldest child and then come Adeline, Harriet, and Texana and Betty before the surrender, and then Henry, Mattie and Louise after it.

When the War come along old Master jest didn't know what to do. He always been taught not to raise his hand up and kill nobody—no matter how come—and he jest kept holding out against all them that was talking about fighting, and he wouldn't go and fight. He been taught that it was all right to have slaves and treat them like he want to, but he been taught it was sinful to go fight and kill to keep them, and he lived up to what he been taught.

They was some Choctaw people lived 'round there, and they flew up and went right off to the War, and Mr. Trot Hand and Mr. Joe Brown that had plantations on the big road towards Quitman both went off with their grown boys right at the start, but old Master was a preacher and he jest stayed out of it. I remember one day I was sent up to the Big House and I heard old Master and some men out at the gate 'xpounding about the War. Some of the men had on soldier clothes, and they acted like they was mad. Somebody tell me later on that they was getting up a home guard because the yankees done got down in Alabama not far away, but old Master wouldn't go in with them.

Two, three days after that, it seems like, old Master come down to the quarters and say git everything bundled up and in the wagons for a long trip. The Negroes all come in and everybody pitch in to help pack up the wagons. Then old Master look around and he can't find Andy. Andy was one Negro that never did act like he been taught, and old Master's patience about wore out with him anyways.

We all know that Andy done run off again, but we didn't know where to. Leastwise all the Negroes tell old Master that. But old Master soon show us we done the work and he done the thinking! He jest goes ahead and keeps all the Negroes busy fixing up the wagons and bundling up the stuff to travel, and keeps us all in his sight all the time, and says nothing about Andy being gone.

Then that night he sends for a white man name Clements that got some blood hounds, and him and Mr. Clements takes time about staying awake and watching all the cabins to see nobody slips out of them. Everybody was afraid to stick their head out.

Early next morning we has all the wagons ready to drive right off, and old Master call Andy's brother up to him. He way, "You go down to that spring and wait, and when Andy come down to the spring to fill that cedar bucket you stole out'n the smokehouse for him to git water in you tell him to come on in here. Tell him I know he is hiding out way down the branch whar he can come up wading the water clean up to the cornfield and the melon patch, so the hounds won't git his scent, but I'm going to send the hounds down there if he don't come on in right now." Then we all knowed we was for the work and old Master was for the thinking, 'cause pretty soon Andy come on in. He'd been right whar old Master think he is.

About that time Mr. Sears come riding down the big road. He was a deacon in old Master's church, and he see us all packed up to leave and so he light at the big gate and walk up to whar we is. He ask old Master where we all lighting out for, and old Master say for Louisiana. We Negroes don't know where that is. Then old deacon say what old Master going to do with Andy, 'cause there stood Mr. Clements holding his blood-hounds and old Master had his cat-o-nine-tails in his hand.

Old Master say just watch him, and he tell Andy if he can make it to that big black gum tree down at the gate before the hounds git him he can stay right up in that tree and watch us all drive off. Then he tell Andy to git!

Poor Andy jest git hold of the bottom limbs when the blood hounds grab him and pull him down onto the ground. Time old Master and Mr. Clements git down there the hounds done tore off all Andy's clothes and bit him all over bad. He was rolling on the ground and holding his shirt up 'round his throat when Mr. Clements git there and pull the hounds off of him.

Then old Master light in on him with that cat-o-nine-tails, and I don't know how many lashes he give him, but he jest bloody all over and done fainted pretty soon. Old Deacon Sears stand it as long as he can and then he step up and grab old Master's arm and say, "Time to stop, Brother! I'm speaking in the name of Jesus!" Old Master quit then, but he still powerful mad. I don't think he believe Andy going to make that tree when he tell him that.

Then he turn on Andy's brother and give him a good beating too, and we all drive off and leave Andy sitting on the ground under a tree and old Deacon standing by him. I don't know what ever become of Andy, but I reckon maybe he went and live with old Deacon Sears until he was free.

When I think back and remember it, it all seems kind of strange, but it seem like old Master and old Deacon both think the same way. They kind of understand that old Master had a right to beat his Negro all he wanted to for running off, and he had a right to set the hounds on him if he did. But he shouldn't of beat him so hard after he told him he was going to let him off if he made the tree, and he ought to keep his word even if Andy was his own slave. That's the way both them white men had been taught, and that was the way they both lived.

Old Master had about five wagons on that trip down into Louisiana, but they was all full of stuff and only the old slaves and children could ride in them. I was big enough to walk most of the time, but one time I walked in the sun so long that I got sick and they put me in the wagon for most the rest of the way.

We would come to places where the people said the Yankees had been and gone, but we didn't run into any Yankees. They was most to the north of us I reckon, because we went on down to the south part of Mississippi and ferried across the big river at Baton Rouge. Then we went on to Lafayette, Louisiana, before we settled down anywhere.

All us Negroes thought that was a mighty strange place. We would hear whitefolks talking and we couldn't understand what they said, and lots of the Negroes talked the same way, too. It was all full of French people around Lafayette, but they had all their menfolks in the Confederate Army just the same. I seen lots of men in butternut clothes coming and going hither and yon, but they wasn't in bunches. They was mostly coming home to see their folks.

Everybody was scared all the time, and two-three times when old Master hired his Negroes out to work the man that hired them quit his place and went on west before they got the crop in. But old Master got a place and we put in a cotton crop, and I think he got some money by selling his place in Mississippi. Anyway, pretty soon after the cotton was all in he moves again and goes to a place on Simonette Lake for the winter. It aint a bit cold in that place, and we didn't have no fire 'cepting to cook, and sometimes a little charcoal fire in some crock pots that the people left on the place when they went on out to Texas.

The next spring old Master loaded up again and we struck out for Texas, when the Yankees got too close again. But Master Bill didn't go to Texas, because the Confederates done come that winter and made him go to the army. I think they took him to New Orleans, and old Master was hopping mad, but he couldn't do anything or they would make him go too, even if he was a preacher.

I think he left out of there partly because he didn't like the people at that place. They wasn't no Baptists around anywheres, and they was all Catholics, and old Master didn't like them.

About that time it look like everybody in the world was going to Texas. When we would be going down the road we would have to walk along the side all the time to let the wagons go past, all loaded with folks going to Texas.

Pretty soon old Master say git the wagons loaded again, and this time we start out with some other people, going north. We go north a while and then turn west, and cross the Sabine River and go to Nachedoches [Nacogdoches], Texas. Me and my brother Joe and my sister Adeline walked nearly all the way, but my little sister Harriet and my mammy rid in a wagon. Mammy was mighty poorly, and jest when we got to the Sabine bottoms she had another baby. Old Master didn't like it 'cause it was a girl, but he named her Texana on account of where she was born and told us children to wait on Mammy good and maybe we would get a little brother next time.

But we didn't. Old Master went with a whole bunch of wagons on out to the prairie country in Coryell County and set up a farm where we just had to break the sod and didn't have to clear off much. And the next baby Mammy had the next year was a girl. We named her Betty because Mistress jest have a baby a little while before and its name was Betty.

Old Master's place was right at the corner where Coryell and Mc-Lennan and Bosque Counties come together, and we raised mostly cotton and jest a little corn for feed. He seem like he changed a lot since we left Mississippi, and seem like he paid more attention to us and looked after us better. But most the people that already live there when we git there was mighty hard on their Negroes. They was mostly hard drinkers and hard talkers, and they work and fight jest as hard as they talk, too!

One day Old Master come out from town and tell us that we all been set free, and we can go or stay jest as we wish. All of my family stay on the place and he pay us half as shares on all we make. Pretty soon the whitefolks begin to cut down on the shares, and the renters git only a third and some less, and the Negroes begin to drift out to other places, but old Master stick to the halves a year or so after that. Then he come down to a third too.

It seems like the white people can't git over us being free, and they do everything to hold us down all the time. We don't git no schools for a long time, and I never see the inside of a school. I jest grow up on hard work. And we can't go 'round where they have the voting, unless we want to ketch a whipping some night, and we have to jest keep on bowing and scraping when we are 'round whitefolks like we did when we was slaves. They had us down and they kept us down. But that was the way they been taught, and I don't blame them for it none, I reckon.

When I git about thirty years old I marry Betty Sadler close to Waco, and we come up to the Creek Nation forty years ago. We come to Muskogee first, and then to Tulsa bout thirty seven years ago.

We had ten children but only seven are alive. Three girls and a boy live here in Tulsa and we got one boy in Muskogee and one at Frederick, Oklahoma.

I sells milk and makes my living, and I keeps so busy I don't think back on the old days much, but if anybody ask me why the Texas Negroes been kept down so much I can tell them. If they set like I did on the bank at that ferry across the Sabine, and see all that long line of covered wagons, miles and miles of them, crossing that river and going west with all they got left out of the War, it aint hard to understand.

Them whitefolks done had everything they had tore up, or had to run away from the places they lived, and they brung their Negroes out to Texas and then right away they lost them too. They always had them Negroes, and lots of them had mighty fine places back in the old states, and then they had to go out and live in sod houses and little old boxed shotguns and turn their Negroes loose. They didn't see no justice in it then, and most of them never did until they died. The folks that stayed at home and didn't straggle all over the country had their old places to live on and their old friends around them, but the Texans was different.

So I says, when they done us the way they did they was jest doing the way they was taught. I don't blame them, because anybody will do that.

Whitefolks mighty decent to me now, and I always tried to teach my children to be respectful and act like they think the whitefolks they dealing with expects them to act. That the way to git along, because some folks been taught one way and some been taught another, and folks always thinks the way they been taught.

Allen V. Manning

. . . .

59

Bob Maynard

❦ ❦ ❦

Age 79 Years
Falls County

I was born near what is now Marlin, Texas, Falls County. My father was Robert Maynard and my mother was Chanie Maynard, both born slaves. Our Master, Gerard Branum, was a very old man and wore long white whiskers. He sho' was a fine built man, and walked straight and tall like a young man.

I was too little to do much work so my job was to carry the key basket for old Mistress. I sho' was proud of that job. The basket held the keys to the pantry, the kitchen, the linen closet, and extra keys to the rooms and smokehouse. When old Mistress started out on her rounds every morning she'd call to me to get de basket and away we'd go. I'd run errands for all the house help too, so I was kept purty busy.

The "big house" was a fine one. It was a big two-story white house made of pine lumber. There was a big porch or veranda across the front and wings on the east and west. The house faced south. There was big round white posts that went clean up to the roof and there was a big porch upstairs too. I believe the house was what you'd call colonial style. There was twelve or fifteen rooms and a big wide stairway. It was a purty place, with a yard and big trees and the house that set in a walnut and pecan grove. They was graveled walks and driveways and all along by the driveway was cedars. There was a hedge close to the house and a flower garden with purty roses, holly hocks and a lot of others I don't know the name of.

Back to the right of the house was the smokehouse, kept full of meat, and further back was the big barns. Old Master kept a spanking pair of carriage horses and several fine riding horses. He kept several pairs of mules, too, to pull the plow. He had some ox teams too.

To the left and back of the "big house" was the quarters. He owned about two thousand acres of land and three hundred slaves. He kept a white overseer and the colored overlooker was my uncle. He sho' saw that the gang worked. He saw to it that the cotton was took to the gin. They used oxen to pull the wagons full of cotton. There was two gins on the plantation. Had to have two for it was slow work to gin a bale of cotton as it was run by horse power.

Old Master raised hundreds of hogs; he raised practically all the food we et. He gave the food out to each family and they done their own cooking except during harvest. The farm hands was fed at the "big house." They was called in from the farm by a big bell.

Sunday was our only day for recreation. We went to church at our own church and we could sing and shout jest as loud as we pleased and it didn't disturb nobody.

During the week after supper we would all set round the doors outside and sing or play music. The only musical instruments we had was a jug or big bottle, a skillet lid or frying pan that they'd hit with a stick or a bone. We had a flute too, made out of reed cane and it'd make good music. Sometimes we'd sing and dance so long and loud old Master'd have to make us stop and go to bed.

The Patrollers, Ku Kluxers or night riders come by sometimes at night to scare the niggers and make 'em behave. Sometimes the slaves would run off and the Patroller would catch 'em and have 'em whipped. I've seen

that done lots of times. They was some wooden stocks (a sort of trough) and they'd put the darky in this and strap him down, take off his clothes and give him 25 to 50 licks, 'cording to what he had done.

I reckon old Master had everything his heart could wish for at this time. Old Mistress was a fine lady and she always went dressed up. She wore long trains on her skirts and I'd walk behind her and hold her train up when she made de rounds. She was awful good to me. I slept on the floor in her little boy's room, and she give me apples and candy just like she did him. Old Master gave ever chick and child good warm clothes for winter. We had store boughten shoes but the women made our clothes. For underwear we all wore "lowers" but no shirts.

After the war started old Master took a lot of his slaves and went to Natchez, Mississippi. He thought he'd have a better chance of keeping us there I guess, and he was afraid we'd be freed and he started running with us. I remember when General Grant blowed up Vicksburg. I had a free born Uncle and Aunt who sometimes visited in the North and they'd tell us how easy it was up there and it sho' made us all want to be free.

I think Abe Lincoln was next to de Lawd. He done all he could for de slaves; he set 'em free. People in the South knowed they'd lose their slaves when he was elected president. 'Fore the election he traveled all over the South and he come to our house and slept in old Mistress' bed. Didn't nobody know who he was. It was a custom to take strangers in and put them up for one night or longer, so he come to our house and he watched close. He seen how the niggers come in on Saturday and drawed four pounds of meat and a peck of meal for a week's rations. He also saw 'em whipped and sold. When he got back up north he writ old Master a letter and told him he was going to have to free his slaves, that everybody was going to have to, that the North was going to see to it. He also told him that he had visited at his house and if he doubted it to go in the same room he slept in and look on the bedstead at the head and he'd see where he'd writ his name. Sho' nuff, there was his name: A. Lincoln.

Didn't none of us like Jeff Davis. We all liked Robert E. Lee, but we was glad that Grant whipped him.

When the War was over, old Master called all the darkies in and lined 'em up in a row. He told 'em they was free to go and do as they pleased. It was six months before any of us left him.

Darkies could vote in Mississippi. Fred Douglas [Frederick Douglass], a colored man, came to Natchez and made political speeches for General Grant.

After the war they was a big steam boat line on the Mississippi River known as the Robert E. Lee Line. They sho' was fine boats too.

We used to have lots of Confederate money. Five cent pieces, two bit pieces, half dollar bills and half dimes. During the war old Master dug a long trench and buried all de silver, fine clothes, jewelry and a lot of money. I guess he dug it up, but I don't remember.

Master died three years after the War. He took it purty good, losing his niggers and all. Lots of men killed theirselves. Old Master was a good old man.

I'm getting old, I reckon. I've been married twice and am the father of 19 chillun. The oldest is 57 and my youngest is two boys, ten and twelve. I had great grandchillun older than them two boys.

Amanda Oliver

❦ ❦ ❦

Age 80 Years
Grayson County

I 'membuh what my mother say—I was born November 9, 1857, in Missouri. I was 'bout eight years old, when she was sold to a master named Harrison Davis. They said he had two farms in Missouri, but when he moved to northern Texas he brought me, my mother, Uncle George, Uncle Dick and a cullud girl they said was 15 with 'im. He owned 'bout 6 acres on de edge of town near Sherman, Texas, and my mother and 'em was all de slaves he had. They said he sold off some of de folks.

We didn't have no overseers in northern Texas, but in southern Texas dey did. Dey didn't raise cotton either; but dey raised a whole lots of corn. Sometime de men would shuck corn all night long. Whenever dey was going to shuck all night de women would piece quilts while de men shuck de corn and you could hear 'em singing and shucking corn. After de cornshucking, de cullud folks would have big dances.

Master Davis lived in a big white frame house. My mother lived in the yard in a big one-room log hut with a brick chimney. De logs was "pinted" (what dey call plastered now with lime). I don't know whether young folks know much 'bout dat sort of thing now.

I slept on de floor up at de "Big House" in de white woman's room on a quilt. I'd git up in de mornings, make fires, put on de coffee, and tend to my little brother. Jest do little odd jobs sech as that.

We ate vegetables from de garden, sech as that. My favorite dish is vegetables now.

I don't remember seeing any slaves sold. My mother said dey sold 'em on de block in Kentucky where she was raised. I don't remembuh when de War broke out, but I remembuh seeing the soldiers with de blue uniforms on. I was afraid of 'em.

Old mistress didn't tell us when we was free, but another white woman told my mother and I remembuh one day old mistress told my mother to git to that wheel and git to work, and my mother said, "I ain't gwineter, I'm just as free as you air." So dat very day my mother packed up all our belongings and moved us to town, Sherman, Texas. She worked awful hard, doing day work for 50¢ a day, and sometimes she'd work for food, clothes or whatever she could git.

I don't believe in conjuring though I heard lotta talk 'bout it. Sometimes I have pains and aches in my hands, feel like sometime dat somebody puts dey hands on me, but I think jest de way my nerves is.

I can't say much 'bout Abe Lincoln. He was a republican in favor of de cullud folk being free. Jeff Davis? Yeah, the boys usta sing a song 'bout 'im:

> *Lincoln rides a fine hoss,*
> *Jeff Davis rides a mule.*
> *Lincoln is de President,*
> *Jeff Davis is de fool.*

Booker T. Washington—I guess he is a right good man. He's for the cullud people I guess.

I been a Christian thirty some odd years. I've been here some thirty odd years. Had to come when my husband died. He died in 1902. We married in 18—I've forgot, but we went to de preacher and got married. We did more than jump over de broom stick.

In those days we went to church with de white folks. Dey had church at eleven and the cullud folks at three, but all of us had white preachers. Our church is standing right there now, at least it was de last time I was there.

I don't have a favorite song, they's so many good ones, but I like, "Bound for the Promised Land." I'm a Baptist, my mother was a Baptist, and her white folks was Baptist.

I have two daughters, Julia Goodwin and Bertha Frazier, and four grandchildren, both of 'ems been separated. Dey do housework.

Noah Perry

🜚 🜚 🜚

Age 81 Years

Old Dixie Land . . .
The land of cotton,
Good times there are not forgotten.

That is the truth all right for I still remember the good and the bad times we had before and just after the war of the rebellion. We had a lot harder time after the war than when we lived wid our old Master. He always looked after us in every way and we didn't have any thing to worry about. We always had plenty to eat and to wear and if we got sick he saw to it that we had plenty of attention and medicine.

I was born in slavery on the plantation of Master William Gore, near Summerville, Georgia. Master William and his wife Miss Sallie owned my mother and my brother and me. My father, Ben Perry, belonged to Squire Perry who owned a plantation about a mile from us. He came to see us often and spent every Saturday night and Sunday wid us. Sometimes he'd come in the middle of the week but as he had to be back on his master's farm so early in the morning to go to work he didn't come very often when the days was short.

Mother and father both had kind masters who never whipped them but looked after them good and give them a good home in return for the work they did for them.

Once father come over to see us. His master didn't care for him coming and he didn't get no pass from him before he left. A patroller got after him and father started running down across the orchard and the patroller right after him. Father ducked under a crooked peach tree and the patroller didn't see it in time and he hit it wid his head and it knocked him out cold. Father didn't stay to see if he got taken care of but went on home. Old Squire Perry gave orders that father was not to be meddled with any more as he didn't have to have a pass. They never did bother him any more.

Mother's rightful owner was Old Man Gore, Master William's father. He had two big plantations and he gave one to Master William and the other to his other son, Master Frank. He give each of his son's a equal number of slaves but always kept a claim on mother and us kids. He had a little house near the big house and when he was visiting Master William he stayed in this little house and mother kept house for him. He usually stayed about six months and we'd get to live at the little house all that time. He thought about as much of me as he did his own grandchildren. Sometimes when they'd get after me to whip me he would take me to his room and keep me away from them. Sometimes he'd make me a pallet and keep me all night. They sure didn't whip me neither. I loved him a lot, too.

When he left to go stay with his son Master Frank[,] mother would put everything to rights and lock up and we'd go back to Master William's to stay till he come back again. Mother liked to stay with him, too, as she didn't have to work so hard there and she was her own boss.

Our white folks lived in a fine house. It was a two-story building facing the south and it had a big gallery across the front and on the east. A big wide hall went clear through the house both upstairs and down and there was rooms on each side of this hall. There was a basement with four rooms in it. The househelp lived down there.

The house set up on a hill and was painted white. You could see it for a long distance. A long winding road lead up to the house from the main big road. There was big shade trees all around the house and the barn. The quarters was below the house about three hundred yards. We had a nice house in the quarters. It was made out of logs but it was well made and had a good floor and was good and warm.

Mother was a good field hand as she was young and strong. She usually run the plow. She liked to plow and made such a good hand at it that the overseer let her plow all the time if she wanted to. She never took much foolishness off any of the other hands neither. One day one of the men got mad at me and whipped me. When she come home of course I told her about it. He went to the barn and hid when he saw her coming. She went out there and drug him out and give him a good thrashing. He never bothered us kids any more either. Mother spanked us good and proper though.

One time I was up at the big house playing with Master William's boys and we got into a fuss about something and I went home. Walter followed me and I run and got over the fence into our yard. Walter climbed on the fence to jump over and I say to him, "Don't you come in this yard, I left your house to keep from fighting and I want you to go on back home." But Walter never paid no attention to what I said and he kept on coming. I picked up a rock and throwed it and hit him right on the fore-head. He fell off that fence just like he was shot off and he just lay there and sort of trembled. I just knowed I'd killed him. Lawsy, I was scared. I run down through the woods lot and hid in some buckeye bushes. I could hear Miss Sallie screaming and saying, "He's killed my Walter, he's killed my Walter." I just laid there and shook. Purty soon here come Master William looking for me. He come so close that I thought sure he could hear my heart beat but he had to give it up. I was afraid to go to the house for I thought they would kill me. Finally mother come home from the field. Master William told her about it and told her she had to whip me. She wanted to know where I was. They told her I was in the woods some-where and she commenced calling me. I decided that if mother was at home she wouldn't let them kill me as she always had taken my part so I went to the house. She sure dusted my britches for me but I didn't mind that like I would have Master William. Walter has that scar till this day if he is still living. We played together after that just like nothing ever happened.

The war come on and times got purty scarey. Master Frank went to the army but Master William didn't. I guess he was too old.

The Yankees come along and took all the able-bodied colored men to the army. Father went as a cook and it was a many long day before we ever saw him again. Our family was all broke up after dat.

Master William took what niggers he had left and refugeed us to Macon, Georgia. Things was so bad in northern Georgia that he decided to stay there, so he took over a place and we raised rice. We stayed there about five years after the war.

Master William decided to go back and see about his old home and he loaded his household goods, tools, niggers, and everything he had onto a freight train and we went back home. The farm was awful run down and all his nigger men and young women quit him so Master William had a hard time rebuilding it. Father had come back after the war and couldn't find us so he married again. Mother and us two boys just stayed on with Master William till I was about fourteen years old. Mother married again and my father come and took me to live with him.

My stepmother had four boys of her own. One of them was grown but the other three were at home with father and her. Her oldest son was a school teacher. They had belonged to a man that taught them all to read and write and even sent the boys to school. He made an awful smart man. I went to school to him and learned all I ever learned at school. I went to another man but I was so scared of him that I couldn't learn. He felt so big that he could teach school that he beat on us kids all the time. He'd make us set on a stool and wear a dunce cap, too. I also went to school to a white teacher that come down from the north. He was smart and I could a learned from him but the Ku Kluxers made him quit teaching us so he went back home.

It was the sorriest day of my life when I went to live with my father. My stepmother just fairly hated me and she done everything she could to make my life a misery to me. She was fairly good to me if father was at home but if he was gone I had an awful time. She wouldn't let me wash my face and hands till her boys all washed. One morning I waited and waited for them to wash and I got tired so I set the pan down in the kitchen door and squatted down to wash. She come up behind me and kicked me out in the yard. Father was out feeding the pigs and he saw it and here he came to the house. I had told him how they treated me but he acted like he hated to believe me but he had to believe his eyes. He come in and cleaned out the whole bunch. This didn't stop them though for every time he left home it was the same thing over again. One day father was gone from home and I done something and she took a big hank of cotton thread and put it around my neck and hung me to a joist. I thought my time had come for I knew there wasn't anybody there that cared whether I lived or died. One of my aunts come up to the back and hollered for my stepmother. She let me down and told me if I told it she would kill me. I believed her and I didn't tell it. I knew she wanted to kill me bad enough. She took sick and died not long after that and that was the only time in my life that I ever said that I was glad that a person was dead. I said it and I sure meant it.

I went back to Master William's to live after that. He give me ten dollars a month and my board to work for him. I stayed with him till I was about twenty-five years old and I married and rented a place for myself.

Bob Perry, one of my stepmother's sons that always seemed to have it in for me worse than any of the boys, married and had two children. His wife died and he had her buried. The day of the funeral he told me, "Noah, I've always wanted to have my way and now I'm gonna do it from now on. You can just mark my words." Well sir, he left that day and none of us ever seen him again. He went off and left his children. My wife and me took his little girl and kept her till she was a grown woman. I tried my best never to be mean to her and I never told her how her grandmother and daddy used to treat me. I think that is one reason that I have always been sort of lucky was that I always tried to be better to people than they was to me.

The country there begun to be thickly settled and I hope [help] my Pappy to buy and pay for 80 acres of land. I took my family and moved to Texas. We didn't stay there but three years and we come to Oklahoma or Indian Territory as it was then.

My wife didn't like it here and I told her she could go back to her mother's if she wanted to[,] that I was going to stay here. We had lost our little girl and just had one child, a boy, so she took him and went back. I been living here by myself ever since. My boy would come out to see me but would go back to his mother. He was killed in France during the World War. My wife is still living.

While I lived in Texas I worked for an old lady named Aunt Patsy Caraway. Every body called her Aunt Patsy. She owned a nice farm and lived by herself. Her family was all dead. She was lonesome and lots of nights my wife and I would go in to her room and set by the fire and listen to her tell of her life in the early days there. She was born in North Carolina she said and married and they come to Texas soon after that. Her husband died when their children was all young and she had to work hard to make a living for them. She was a little woman[;] I don't suppose she would weigh more than 115 or 120 pounds. A lot of the things she told us seemed kind of hard to believe but I guess they was true[;] any way I will tell you what she told me and you can take it or leave it.

She and her husband had settled on a place and started to improve it. They were doing very well and her husband took sick and after a long time he died. She had no one to help her with making a living for her children so she just worked harder. She had a few head of cattle that had a free range and she also had some hogs that had free range. She lived close to a swamp and the hogs did well on the mast. The hogs raised themselves in the woods and she always had plenty of meat, milk and butter. She also raised lots of bees and they had honey the year round. They raised corn for bread and used honey for sugar as they didn't know what it was to have coffee or sugar or flour. She usually had honey to sell and they spun and wove their clothes. By every body working they managed to keep going.

Her farm lay at the edge of a big swamp and was about fifteen or twenty miles from Beaumont, Texas. This swamp was a regular jungle and she had some of it cleared and had her farm there. She had about twenty acres cleared and in cultivation. The house set back on a hill. She said wild be[a]sts of almost every kind ranged the swamps at the time they settled there and you could believe it, too, as it looked plenty wild then. Black bear was plentiful. They feasted on her young calves and pigs and she had a hard time with them. One day she said the dogs began to bark and run as if something terrible was around and she took her gun and kept mooching them along till finally they came to bay down in the swamp. She went on to see what they had and found a big black bear. She shot it and butchered it and brought it home. She had to make several trips on horseback and found a ready sale for it at a good price. She always made the trip to town in one day, always on horseback and carried whatever she had for sale. She said that once she even took her churn full of milk and churned it as she rode along the road. When she got to Beaumont her churning was done so she sold her butter and milk and returned home that evening with whatever produce she needed.

She said that one night she heard something out in the yard and she went out to see what it was. She went to the smokehouse door and she saw a Mexican lion [puma] in the smokehouse. It gave a loud scream and run out the door past her and was so scared that it kept on running. I asked her if she wasn't afraid and she said, "Afraid, what is that? I never saw one of them things. I couldn't afford to be afraid for I was the man and the woman of the family."

I left there and come to the mines at Krebs and I been here ever since. I never had no trouble till just here lately. A boy was living here with me and we got along good for he was a good boy. He was keeping company with one of my nieces.

One night I was setting here by the fire and he come running in and said, "Uncle Noah, let me have your gun, quick!" I said, "I can't let you have my gun, you might kill somebody." He said, "That's just what I want it for, so let me have it." I always kept it leaning against the wall behind the door and he grabbed it and started by me and I grabbed hold of it and told him that I couldn't let him have my gun to kill anybody[,] that I'd be just as guilty as he was and besides he didn't need to kill anybody. He kept jerking on the gun, a shotgun, and I kept holding on to it. He give a big jerk and it went off and shot him in the stomach and killed him right then. They arrested me and I stayed in jail for 24 days. The good Lord knows that I didn't kill him. We was good friends and besides I wouldn't a killed nobody. My lawyer says he don't think it ever will come up any more but I just worry about it all the time. I never had no trouble in my young days and it looks hard for me to have this to worry about in my old days. I bought me a Bible and I reads it a lot. I ain't never been converted but I wants to be.

Phyllis Petite

☙ ☙ ☙

Age 83 Years
Rusk County

I was born in Rusk County, Texas, on a plantation about eight miles east of Belleview [Bellview]. There wasn't no town where I was born, but they had a church.

My mammy and pappy belonged to a part Cherokee named W. P. Thompson when I was born. He had kinfolks in the Cherokee Nation, and we all moved up here to a place on Fourteen-Mile Creek close to where Hulbert now is, 'way before I was big enough to remember anything. Then, so I been told, old master Thompson sell my pappy and mammy and one of my baby brothers and me back to one of his neighbors in Texas name of John Harnage.

Mammy's name was Letitia Thompson and pappy's was Riley Thompson. My little brother was named Johnson Thompson, but I had another brother sold to a Vann and he always call hisself Harry Vann. His Cherokee master lived on the Arkansas river close to Webber's Falls and I never did know him until we was both grown. My only sister was Patsy and she was borned after slavery and died at Wagoner, Oklahoma.

I can just remember when Master John Harnage took us to Texas. We went in a covered wagon with oxen and camped out all along the way. Mammy done the cooking in big wash kettles and pappy done the driving of the oxen. I would set in a wagon and listen to him pop his whip and holler.

Master John took us to his plantation and it was a big one, too. You could look from the field up to the Big House and any grown body in the yard look like a little body, it was so far away.

We negroes lived in quarters not far from the Big House and ours was a single log house with a stick and dirt chimney. We cooked over the hot coals in the fireplace.

I just played around until I was about six years old I reckon, and then they put me up at the Big House with my mammy to work. She done all the cording and spinning and weaving, and I done a whole lot of sweeping and minding the baby. The baby was only about six months old I reckon. I used to stand by the cradle and rock it all day, and when I quit I would go to sleep right by the cradle sometimes before mammy would come and get me.

The Big House had great big rooms in front, and they was fixed up nice, too. I remember when old Mistress Harnage tried me out sweeping up the front rooms. They had two or three great big pictures of some old people hanging on the wall. They was full blood Indians it look like, and I was sure scared of them pictures! I would go here and there and every which-a-way, and anywheres I go them big pictures always looking straight at me and watching me sweep! I kept my eyes right on them so I could run if they moved, and old Mistress take me back to the kitchen and say I can't sweep because I miss all the dirt.

We always have good eating, like turnip greens cooked in a kettle with hog skins and crackling grease, and skinned corn, and rabbit or possum stew. I liked big fish tolerable well too, but I was afraid of the bones in the little ones.

That skinned corn aint like the boiled hominy we have today. To make it you boil some wood ashes, or have some drip lye from the hopper to put in the hot water. Let the corn boil in the lye water until the skin drops off and the eyes drop out and then wash that corn in fresh water about a dozen times, or just keep carrying water from the spring until you are wore out, like I did. Then you put the corn in a crock and set it in the spring, and you got good skinned corn as long as it last, all ready to warm up a little batch at a time.

Master had a big, long log kitchen setting away from the house, and we set a big table for the family first, and when they was gone we negroes at the house eat at that table too, but we don't use the china dishes.

The negro cook was Tilda Chisholm. She and my mammy didn't do no outwork. Aunt Tilda sure could make them corn-dodgers. Us children would catch her eating her dinner first out of the kettles and when we say something she say: "Go on child, I jest tasting that dinner."

In the summer we had cotton homespun clothes, and in winter it had wool mixed in. They was dyed with copperas and wild indigo.

My brother, Johnson Thompson, would get up behind old Master Harnage on his horse and go with him to hunt squirrels[; Johnson would go 'round on the other side of the tree and rock the squirrels] so they would go 'round on Master's side so's he could shoot them. Master's old mare was named "Old Willow," and she knowed when to stop and stand real still so he could shoot.

His children was just all over the place! He had two houses full of

them! I only remember Bell, Ida, Maley, Mary and Will, but they was plenty more I don't remember.

That old horn blowed 'way before daylight, and all the field negroes had to be out in the row by the time of sun up. House negroes got up too, because old Master always up to see everybody get out to work.

Old Master Harnage bought and sold slaves most all the time, and some of the new negroes always acted up and needed a licking. The worst ones got beat up good, too! They didn't have no jail to put slaves in because when the Masters got done licking them they didn't need no jail.

My husband was George Petite. He tell me his mammy was sold away from him when he was a little boy. He looked down a long lane after her just as long as he could see her, and cried after her. He went down to the big road and set down by his mammy's barefooted tracks in the sand and set there until it got dark, and then he come on back to the quarters.

I just saw one slave try to get away right in hand. They caught him with bloodhounds and brung him back in. The hounds had nearly tore him up, and he was sick a long time. I don't remember his name, but he wasn't one of the old regular negroes.

In Texas we had a church where we could go. I think it was a white church and they just let the negroes have it when they got a preacher sometimes. My mammy took me sometimes, and she loved to sing them salvation songs.

We used to carry news from one plantation to the other I reckon, 'cause mammy would tell about things going on [at] some other plantation and I know she never been there.

Christmas morning we always got some brown sugar candy or some molasses to pull, and we children was up bright and early to get that 'lasses pull, I tell you! And in the winter we played skeeting on the ice when the water froze over. No, I don't mean skating. That's when you got iron skates, and we didn't have them things. We just get a running start and jump on the ice and skeet as far as we could go, and then you run some more.

I nearly busted my head open, and brother Johnson said: "Try it again," but after that I was scared to skeet any more.

Mammy say we was down in Texas to get away from the War, but I didn't see any war and any soldiers. But one day old Master stay after he eat breakfast and when us negroes come in to eat he say: "After today I ain't your master any more. You all as free as I am." We just stand and look and don't know what to say about it.

After while pappy got a wagon and some oxen to drive for a white man who was coming to the Cherokee Nation because he had folks here. His name was Dave Mounts and he had a boy named John.

We come with them and stopped at Fort Gibson where my own grand mammy was cooking for the soldiers at the garrison. Her name was Phyllis Brewer and I was named after her. She had a good Cherokee master. My mammy was born on his place.

We stayed with her about a week and then we moved out on Four Mile Creek to live. She died on Fourteen-Mile Creek about a year later.

When we first went to Four Mile Creek I seen negro women chopping wood and asked them who they work for and I found out they didn't know they was free yet.

After a while my pappy and mammy both died, and I was took care of by my aunt Elsie Vann. She took my brother Johnson too, but I don't know who took Harry Vann.

I was married to George Petite, and I had on a white underdress and black high-top shoes, and a large cream colored hat, and on top of all I had a blue wool dress with tassels all around the bottom of it. That dress was for me to eat the terrible supper in. That what we called the wedding supper because we eat too much of it. Just danced all night, too! I was at Mandy Foster's house in Fort Gibson, and the preacher was Reverend Barrows. I had that dress a long time, but its gone now. I still got the little sun bonnet I wore to church in Texas.

We had six children, but all are dead but George, Tish, and Annie now.

Yes, they tell me Abraham Lincoln set me free, and I love to look at his picture on the wall in the school house at Four Mile branch where they have church. My grand mammy kind of help start that church, and I think everybody ought to belong to some church.

I want to say again my Master Harnage was Indian, but he was a good man and mighty good to us slaves, and you can see I am more than six feet high and they say I weighs over a hundred and sixty, even if my hair is snow white.

Alice Rawlings

❦ ❦ ❦

Age 80 Years
Cass County

My mother, Tishea Mickens, was sold to an owner in Virginia just a little while after I was born, and I didn't see her for a long time, not until old Master Major Jackson bought her back and kept her till the freedom come.

My mistress Lucy told me I was born on February 1, 1858, near Linden, Cash [Cass] County, Texas. My father was Jack Mickens, the hardest working slave on Major Jackson's Texas plantation. He was the blacksmith and even before the slaves was made free my father earned outside money that his master allowed him to keep. He had money when he was set free.

Father was born in Montgomery, Alabama. There was seven of us children but I forgot the names of all but my brother Albert Mickens who lives down in Texas somewheres to this day.

Major Jackson had two plantations, one in Texas and the other in Alabama. Guess he moved from that country to Texas when the war come along.

His house was a large one and it was about 10-mile from the river dock. I was born in his house. There was a big smokehouse, and plenty of hogs was killed to keep it full. He had the men kill beef and dry it out, and everybody had good things to eat all the time.

There was lots of overseers around the plantation; folks said there was about 6,000-acre of the place and it took lots of work to keep it going. It was all cleared by slaves, just land, good farm land made right from under the trees they chopped down.

A long time after slavery was over, just about the time I had three children of my own I saw the old place again. It was still standing. We was traveling through the country and Lord! I look around and over from the road about a mile was the old house setting lonesome on a little hill. But the Major and the Mistress was no more, they gone to Heaven I know, because they was both good folks.

I heard talk about the war times. About Vicksburg. How it was a terrible fight, and how General Pemberton give up his sword to General Grant, and everybody said that was the turning point of victory for the North Yankees. My father said General Grant laid siege for 47 days in 1863, but that's all I remember.

Saturday night, according to what my paw told me, was negro night. The slaves could get passes and go to town. The white folks seems like didn't go out on that night, just leave it to the negroes and they've still got the habit of parading around the streets on Saturday nights.

The Master Major had one boy who went off to the war. Took some of his own slaves with him. They took good care of that boy because he come through the war without getting even hurt and all the negroes was happy when he come on the Texas place.

The war was over then. But slavery wasn't. No, the old master didn't tell us about freedom until after the crops was in and made. Six months after all the rest was free.

Master's place was called Elms Court and the plantation next to his was owned by a friendly planter. He talked with my father in the road one day. Before we all knew that the other slaves was freed. I guess that's how we heard about it.

The white man asked pa why don't you buy your own land? But pa told though he had saved a little money it wouldn't go far enough to buy a farm and mules and plows and such, for when it come to buying his own rations and clothes for all the children there wouldn't be much left to save for a farm.

The Major was sick when they finally told us about the freedom. His son James was back from the war and he seemed glad for us to know about [it]. So did his sister, Liza, and another girl who I done forgot her name.

One time during the war some of the Yankee soldiers come to the place. The Major knew they was coming and he locked up the house, made everybody hide out. He was hiding too. Them soldiers look around and found my mother. She was the cook. They stack their guns on the porch, feed their horses and water them and tell my mother to start cooking. She said she never cook so much before in all her life.

Some of the slaves come out from hiding places and the soldiers told them to take all the food stuffs they wanted. My father told the negroes not to touch the master stuff and just one negro stole a ham, and she was my aunt who said she just had to have some lean meat.

My uncle Amos worked in the tanyard. He got sick one evening but the overseer didn't think he was so bad off but the next morning he was dead. The master fix up a box to bury him and all the children sat around and cried.

My mother was kinder mean sometimes, and wasn't scared of overseers or nothing. One time when she was working on the master's Alabama place an overseer tried to shoot her. She grabbed the gun and run for the river. She dropped the gun in the river and the overseer got over his temper and left her alone.

There was another overseer on the place that was terrible mean. That's what my folks said about him. If a slave done something to make him mad that man would burn their nose or their ears with fire brands. I saw some of them who had their ears burned nearly off.

The slaves was allowed to go to church. Set in a corner away in the back of the building. Some of the old people could leave to stay at home for washing their clothes on Sunday. That was the only thing keep 'em out of church.

Well, I had another uncle who was a runaway. They said he was never caught. Like another slave the master bought once. He run away too. He didn't like the Major and one day he said, "I won't serve you, just put me in your pocket." He meant for the master to sell him. Then he ran for a hideout. The overseers found him in a boat hull and they near cut him to pieces. An old negro woman greased him every morning and he got well.

Then he run off again. This time he got away and wrote to the master a long time after bragging how the master couldn't get him now because he was in a free state.

My first husband was Thomas Pepper, the second was Eliza Henry. They was just husbands by agreement but the last one, John Rawlings, I married him. Got three children—Carrie, Harrison and Joe.

I belong to the Methodist church and I think all should be religious. The Lord done helped us [out of] slavery[;] now it's our turn to help the Lord. That's the way I feel about it.

Red Richardson

❦ ❦ ❦

Age 75 Years
Grimes County

I was born July 21, 1862, at Grimes County, Texas. Smith Richardson was my father's name, and Eliza Richardson was my mother's. My father came from Virginia. My mother was born in Texas.

We lived in so many places round there I can't tell jest what, but we lived in a log house most of the time. We slept on the flo' on pallets on one quilt. We ate cornbread, beans, vegetables, and got to drink plenty milk. We ate rabbits, fish, possums and such as that but we didn't get no chicken. I don't have no fav'rite food, I don't guess.

We wore shirts, long shirts slit up the side. I didn't know what pants was until I was 14. In Grimes County it ain't even cold these days, and I never wore no shoes. I married in a suit made of broad cloth. It had a tail on the coat.

Master Ben Hadley, and Mistress Minnie Hadley, they had three sons: John, Henry and Charley. Didn't have no overseer. We had to call all white folks, poor or rich, Master and Mistress. Master Hadley owned 'bout 2,000 acres. He had a big number of slaves. They used to wake 'em up early in the mornings by ringing a large bell. They said they used to whip 'em, drive 'em, and sell 'em away from their chillun,—I'd hear my old folks talk about it. Say they wasn't no such thing as going to jail. The master stood good for anything his nigger done. If the master's nigger killed 'im another nigger, the old master stood good.

They never had no schools for the Negro chillun. I can't remember the date of the first school—its in a book someplace—but anyway I went to one of the first schools that was established for the education of Negro chillun.

You know Mr. Negro always was a church man, but he don't mean nothing. I don't have no fav'rite spiritual. All of them's good ones. Whenever they'd baptize they'd sing:

"Harp from the Tune the Domeful Sound."

Which starts like this:

> *Come live in man and view this ground*
> *where we must sho'ly lie.*

I'm a member of Tabernacle Baptist Church myself, and I think all people should be religious 'cause Jesus died for us all.

The patrollers used to run after me but I'd jump 'em. They used to have [to have] a permit to go from one plantation to another. You had to go to old master and say, "I want to go to such and such a place." And if you had a permit they didn't bother you. The patroller would stop you and say, "Where you going? You got a permit to go to such and such a place?" You'd say, yes suh, and show that pass. Den he wouldn't bother you and iffen he did old Master would git on 'em.

When 10:00 o'clock come which was bed time the slaves would go to their cabins and some of 'em would go stealing chickens, hogs, steal sweet potatoes, and cook and eat 'em. Jest git in to all kind of devilment.

Old Master would give 'em Sadday afternoon off, and they'd have them Sadday breakdowns. We played a few games such as marbles, mumble peg, and cards—jest anything to pass off the time. Heahs one of the games we'd play an' I sho did like it too:

> *She is my sweetheart as I stan'.*
> *Come an' stan' beside me,*
> *Kiss her sweet an'*
> *Hug her near.*

On Christmas they'd make egg nog, drink whiskey and kiss their girls.

Wore some charms to ward off the devil, but I don't believe in such. I do believe in voodoo like this: People can put propositions up to you and fool you. Don't believe in ghost. Tried to see 'em but I never could.

Old master didn't turn my father loose and tell 'em we was free. They didn't turn us loose 'til they got the second threat from President Lincoln. Good old Lincoln; they was nothing like 'im. Booker T. Washington was one of the finest Negro Educators in the world, but old Jefferson Davis was against the cullud man.

I think since slavery is all over, it has been a benefit to the cullud man. He's got more freedom now.

Harriett Robinson

❦ ❦ ❦

Age 95 Years
Bastrop County

I was born September 1, 1842, in Bastrop, Texas, on Colorado River. My pappy was named Harvey Wheeler and my mammy was named Carolina Sims. My brothers and sisters was named Alex, Taylor, Mary, Cicero, Tennessee, Sarah, Jeff, Ella and Nora. We lived in cedar log houses with dirt floors and double chimneys, and doors hung on wooden hinges. One side of our beds was bored in the walls and had one leg on the other. Them white folks give each nigger family a blanket in winter.

I nussed 3 white chillun, Lulu, Helen Augusta, and Lola Sims. I done this before that War that set us free. We kids use to make extra money by toting gravel in our aprons. They'd give us dimes and silver nickels.

Our clothes was wool and cotton mixed. We had red rustic [russet] shoes, soles one-half inch thick. They'd go a-whick a-whack. The mens had pants wid one seam and a right-hand pocket. Boys wore shirts.

We ate hominy, mush, grits and pone bread for the most part. Many of them ate out of one tray with wooden spoons. All vittles for field hands was fixed together.

Women broke in mules[,] throwed 'em down and roped 'em. They'd do it better'n men. While mammy made some hominy one day both my foots was scalded and when they clipped them blisters, they just put some cotton round them and catched all dat yellow water and made me a yellow dress out of it. This was 'way back yonder in slavery, before the War.

Whenever white folks had a baby born den all de old niggers had to come thoo the room and the master would be over 'hind the bed and he'd say, "Here's a new little mistress or master you got to work for." You had to say, "Yessuh Master" and bow real low or the overseer would crack you. Them was slavery days, dog days.

I remember in slavery time we had stages. Them devilish things had jest as many wrecks as cars do today. One thing, we jest didn't have as many.

My mammy belonged to Master Colonel Sims and his old mean wife

Julia. My pappy belonged to Master Meke Smith and his good wife Harriett. She was sho' a good woman. I was named after her. Master Sam and Master Meke was partners. Ever year them rich men would send so many wagons to New Mexico for different things. It took 6 months to go and come.

Slaves was punished by whip and starving. Decker was sho' a mean slave-holder. He lived close to us. Master Sam didn't never whip me, but Miss Julia whipped me every day in the mawning. During the war she beat us so terrible. She say, "You master's out fighting and losing blood trying to save you from them Yankees, so you kin git your'n here." Miss Julia would take me by my ears and butt my head against the wall. She wanted to whip my mother, but old Master told her, naw sir. When his father done give my mammy to Master Sam, he told him not to beat her, and iffen he got to whar he just had to, jest bring her back and place her in his yard from whar he got her.

White folks didn't 'low you to read or write. Them what did know come from Virginny. Mistress Julia used to drill her chillun in spelling any words. At every word them chillun missed, she gived me a lick 'cross the head for it. Meanest woman I ever seen in my whole life.

This skin I got now, it ain't my first skin. That was burnt off when I was a little child. Mistress used to have a fire made on the fireplace and she made me scour the brass round it and my skin jest blistered. I jest had to keep pulling it off'n me.

We didn't had no church, though my pappy was a preacher. He preached in the quarters. Our baptizing song was "On Jordan's Stormy Bank I Stand" and "Hark from the Tomb." Now all dat was before the War. We had all our funerals at the graveyard. Everybody, chillun and all picked up a clod of dirt and throwed in on top the coffin to help fill up the grave.

Talking 'bout niggers running away, didn't my step-pappy run away? Didn't my uncle Gabe run away? The frost would jest bite they toes most nigh off too, whiles they was gone. They put Uncle Isom (my step-pappy) in jail and while's he was in there he killed a white guardman. Then they put him in the paper, "A nigger to kill," and our Master seen it and bought him. He was a double-strengthed man, he was so strong. He'd run off so help you God. They had the blood hounds after him once and he caught the hound what was leading and beat the rest of the dogs. The white folks run up on him before he knowed it and made them dogs eat his ear plumb out. But don't you know he got away anyhow. One morning I was sweeping out the hall in the big house and somebody come a-knocking on the front door and I goes to the door. There was Uncle Isom wid rags all on his head. He said, "Tell old master heah I am." I goes to Master's door and says, "Master Colonel Sam, Uncle Isom said heah eh am." He say, "[Well, well, Mr. Isom, thought you was dead.] Go 'round to the kitchen and tell black mammy to give you breakfast." When he was thoo' eating they give him 300 lashes and, bless my soul, he run off again.

When we went to a party the nigger fiddlers would play a chune dat went lak this:

I fooled Old Mastah 7 years
Fooled the overseer three;
Hand me down my banjo
And I'll tickle your bel–lee.

We had the same doctors the white folks had and we wore asafetida and garlic and onions to keep from taking all them ailments.

I 'member the battle being fit. The white folks buried all the jewelry and silver and all the gold in the Blue Ridge Mountains [?], in Orange [?], Texas. Master made all us niggers come together and git ready to leave 'cause the Yankees was coming. We took a steamer. Now this was in slavery time, sho' 'nuff slavery. Then we got on a steamship and pulled out to Galveston. Then he told the captain to feed we niggers. We was on the bay, not the ocean. We left Galveston and went on trains for Houston.

One, my sister Liza, was mulatto and Master Colonel Simms' son had 3 chillun by her. We never seen her no more after her last child was born. I found out though that she was in Canada.

After the War, Master Colonel Sims went to git the mail and so he call Daniel Ivory, the overseer, and say to him, "Go round to all the quarters and tell all them niggers to come up, I got a paper to read to 'em. They're free now, so you kin git you another job, 'cause I ain't got no more niggers which is my own." Niggers come up from the cabins nappy-headed, jest lak they gwine to the field. Master Colonel Sims say, "Caroline (that's my mammy), you is free as me. Pa said bring you back and I'se gwina do jest that. So you go on and work and I'll pay you and your three oldest chillun $10.00 a monthly a head and $4.00 for Harriet[t]," that's me, and then he turned to the rest and say "Now all you'uns will receive $10.00 a head till the crops is laid by." Don't you know before he got half way thoo,' over half them niggers was gone.

Them Klu Klux Klans come and ask for water with their false stomachs and make lak they was drinking three bucketsful. They done some terrible things, but God seen it all and marked it down.

We didn't had no law, we had "bureau." Why, in them days iffen somebody stole anything from you, they had to pay you and not the Law. Now they done turned that round and you don't git nothing.

One day whiles master was gone hunting, Mistress Julia told her brother to give Miss Harriett (me) a free whipping. She was a nigger killer. Master Colonel Sam come home and he said, "You infernal sons o' bitches don't you know there is 300 Yankees camped out here and iffen they knowed you whipped this nigger the way you done done, they'd kill all us. Iffen they find it out, I'll kill all of you." Old rich devils, I'm here, but they is gone.

God choosed Abraham Lincoln to free us. It took one of them to free us so's they couldn't say nothing.

Doing one 'lection they sung:

> *Clark et the watermelon*
> *J. D. Giddings et the vine!*
> *Clark gone to Congress*
> *An' J. D. Giddings left behind.*

They hung Jeff Davis up a sour apple tree. They say he was a president, but he wasn't, he was a big senator man.

Booker T. Washington was all right in his way, I guess, but Bruce and Fred Douglass, or big mens jest sold us back to the white folks.

I married Haywood Telford and had 13 chillun by him. My oldest daughter is the mammy of 14. All my chillun but four done gone to heaven before me.

I jined the church in Chapel Hill, Texas. I am born of the Spirit of God sho' nuff. I played with him seven years and would go right on dancing at Christmas time. Now I got religion. Everybody oughta live right, though you won't have no friends iffen you do.

Our overseer was a poor man. Had us up before day and lak-a-that. He was paid to be the head of punishment. I jest didn't like to think of them old slavery days, dogs' days.

Andrew Simms

❦ ❦ ❦

Age 80 Years
Freestone County

My parents come over on a slave ship from Africa about twenty year before I was born on the William Driver plantation down in Florida. My folks didn't know each other in Africa but my old Mammy told me she was captured by Negro slave hunters over there and brought to some coast town where the white buyers took her and carried her to America.

She was kinder a young gal then and was sold to some white folks when the boat landed here. Dunno who they was. The same thing happened to my pappy. Must have been about the same time from the way they tells it. Maybe they was on the same boat, I dunno.

They was traded around and then mammy was sold to William Driver. The plantation was down in Florida. Another white folks had a plantation close by. Mister Simms was the owner. Bill Simms—that's the name pappy kept after the War.

Somehow or other mammy and pappy meets 'round the place and the first thing happens they is in love. That's what mammy say. And the next thing happen is me. They didn't get married. The Master's say it is alright for them to have a baby. They never gets married, even after the War. Just jumped the broomstick and goes to living with somebody else I reckon.

Then when I was four year old along come the War and Master Driver takes up his slaves and leaves the Florida country and goes way out to Texas. Mammy goes along, I goes along, all the children goes along. I don't remember nothing about the trip but I hears mammy talk about it when I gets older.

Texas, that was the place, down near Fairfield. That's where I learn to do the chores. But the work was easy for the Master was kind as old Mammy herself and he never give me no hard jobs that would wear me down. All the slaves on our place was treated good. All the time. They didn't whip. The Master feeds all the slaves on good clean foods and lean meats so's they be strong and healthy.

Master Driver had four children, Mary, Julia, Frank and George. Every one of them children kind and good just [like] the old Master. They was never mean and could I find some of 'em now hard times would leave me on the run! They'd help this old man get catched up on his eating!

Makes me think of the old song we use to sing:

> *Don't mind working from Sun to Sun,*
> *Iffen you give me my dinner—*
> *When the dinner time comes!*

Nowadays I gets me something to eat when I can catch it. The trouble is sometimes I don't catch! But that ain't telling about the slave days.

In them times it was mostly the overseers and the drivers who was the mean ones. They caused all the misery. There was other whitefolks caused troubles too. Sneak around where there was lots of the black children on the plantation and steal them. Take them poor children away off and sell them.

There wasn't any Sunday Schooling. There was no place to learn to read and write—no big brick schools like they is now. The old Master say we can teach ourselves but we can't do it. Old Elam Bowman owned the place next door to Mister Driver. If he catch his slaves toying with the pencil, why, he cut off one of their fingers. Then I reckon they lost interest in education and get their mind back on the hoe and plow like he say for them to do.

I didn't see no fighting during of the War. If they was any Yankees soldiering around the country I don't remember nothing of it.

Long time after the War is over, about 1885, I meets a gal named Angeline. We courts pretty fast and gets married. The wedding was a sure enough affair with the preacher saying the words just like the whitefolks marriage. We is sure married.

The best thing we do after that is raise us a family. One of them old fashioned families. Big 'uns! Seventeen children does we have and twelve of them still living. Wants to know they names? I ain't never forgets a one! There was Lucy, Bill, Ebbie, Cora, Minnie, George, Frank, Kizzie, Necie, Andrew, Joe, Sammie, David, Fannie, Jacob, Bob and Myrtle.

All good children. Just like their old pappy who's tried to care for 'em just like the old Master takes care of their old daddy when he was a boy on that plantation down Texas way.

When the age comes on a man I reckon religion gets kind of meanful. Thinks about it mor'n when he's young and busy in the fields. I believes in the Bible and what it says to do. Some of the Colored folks takes to the voodoo. I don't believe in it. Neither does I believe in the fortune telling or charms. I aims to live by the Bible and leave the rabbit foots alone!

Liza Smith

❦ ❦ ❦

Age 91 Years
McLennan County

Both my mammy and pappy was brought from Africa on a slave boat and sold on de Richmond (Va.) slave market. What year dey come over I don't know. My mammy was Jane Mason, belonging to Frank Mason; pappy was Frank Smith, belonging to a master wid de same name. I mean, my pappy took his Master's name, and den after my folks married mammy took de name of Smith, but she stayed on wid de Masons and never did belong to my pappy's master. Den, after Frank Mason took all his slaves out of de Virginia count[r]y, mammy met up wid another man, Ben Humphries, and married him.

In Richmond, dat's where I was born, 'bout 1847, de Master said; and dat make me more dan 90-year old dis good year. I had two brothers named Webb and Norman, a half-brother Charley, and two half-sisters, Mealey and Ann. Me, I was born a slave and so was my son. His father, Toney, was one of de Mason slave boys; de Master said I was 'bout 13-year old when de boy was born.

Frank Mason was a young man when de War started, living wid his mother. Dey had lots of slaves, maybe a hundred, and dey always try to take good care of 'em; even after de War was over he worried 'bout trying to get us settled so's we wouldn't starve. De Master had overseer, but dere was no whuppings.

All de way from Richmond to a place dey call Waco, Texas, we traveled by ox-wagon and boats, and den de Master figures we all be better off over in Arkansas and goes to Pine Bluff.

What wid all de running 'round de slaves was kept clean and always wid plenty to eat and good clothes to wear. De Master was plenty rich man and done what his mother, Mis Betty Mason, told him when we all left de Big Mansion, way back dere in Richmond. De Mistress say, "Frank, you watch over dem Negroes cause dey's good men and women; keep dem clean!" Dat's what he done, up until we was freed, and den times was so hard nobody wanted us many Negroes around, and de work was scarce, too. Hard times! Folks don't know what hard times is.

When a Negro get sick de master would send out for herbs and roots. Den one of de slaves who knew how to cook and mix 'em up for medicine use would give de doses. All de men and women wore charms, something like beads, and if dey was any good or not I don't know, but we didn't have no bad diseases like after dey set us free.

I was at Pine Bluff when de Yankees was shooting all over de place. De fighting got so hot we all had to leave; dat's the way it was all de time for us during de War—running away to some place or de next place, and we was all glad when it stopped and we could settle down in a place.

We was back at Waco when de peace come, but Master Frank was away from home when dat happen. It was on a Sunday when he got back and called all de slaves up in de yard and counted all of dem, young and old.

The first thing he said was, "You men and women is all free! I'm going back to my own mammy in old Virginia, but I ain't going back until all de old people is settled in cabins and de young folks fix up wid tents!"

Den he kinder stopped talking. Seem now like he was too excited to talk, or maybe he was feeling bad and worried 'bout what he going to do wid all of us. Pretty soon he said, "You men and women, can't none of you tell anybody I ain't always been a good master. Old folks, have I ever treated you mean?" he asked. Everybody shout, "No, sir!" And Master Frank smiled; den he told us he was going 'round and find places for us to live.

He went to see Jim Tinsley, who owned some slaves, about keeping us. Tinsley said he had cabins and could fix up tents for extra ones, if his own Negroes was willing to share up with us. Dat was the way it worked out. We stayed on dere for a while, but times was so hard we finally get dirty and ragged like all de Tinsley Negroes. But Master Frank figure he done the best he could for us.

After he go back to Virginia we never hear no more of him, but every day I still pray if he has any folks in Richmond dey will find me someway before I die. Is dere someway I could find dem, you s'pose?

Lou Smith

☃ ☃ ☃

Age 83 Years

Sho,' I remembers de slavery days! I was a little gal but I can tell you lots of things about dem days. My job was nussing de younguns. I took keer of them from daylight to dark. I'd have to sing them to sleep too. I'd sing:

> *By-lo Baby Bunting*
> *Daddy's gone a-hunting*
> *To get a rabbit skin*
> *To wrap Baby Bunting in.*

Sometimes I'd sing:

> *Rock-a-bye baby, in a tree top*
> *When de wind blows your cradle'll rock.*
> *When de bough breaks de crad'll fall*
> *Down comes baby cradle'n all.*

My father was Jackson Longacre and he was born in Mississippi. My mother, Caroline, was born in South Carolina. Both of them was born slaves. My father belonged to Huriah Longacre. He had a big plantation and lots of niggers. He put up a lot of his slaves as security on a debt and he took sick and died so they put them all on de block and sold them. My father and his mother (my grandma) was sold together. My old Mistress bought my grandmother and old Mistress' sister bought my grandma's sister. These white women agreed that they would never go off so far that the two slave women couldn't see each other. They allus kept this promise. A Mr. Covington offered old Master $700 for me when I was about ten years old, but he wouldn't sell me. He didn't need to for he was rich as cream and my, how good he was to us.

Young Master married Miss Jo Arnold and old Master sent me and my mother over to live with them. I was small when I was took out from old man McWilliams' yard. It was his wife that bought my grandmother and my father. My mother's folks always belonged to his family.

They all moved to Texas and we all lived there until after the surrender.

Miss Jo wasn't a good Mistress and mother and me wasn't happy. When young Master was there he made her treat us good but when he was gone she made our lives a misery to us. She was what we called a "low-brow." She never had been used to slaves and she treated us like dogs. She said us kids didn't need to wear any clothes and one day she told us we could jest take 'em off as it cost too much to clothe us. I was jest a little child but I knowed I oughten to go without any clothes. We wore little enough as it was. In summer we just wore one garment, a sort of slip without any sleeves. Well, anyway, she made me take off my clothes and I just crept off and cried. Purty soon young Master come home.

He wanted to know what on earth I was doing without my dress on. I told him, and my goodness, but he raised the roof. He told her if she didn't treat us better he was going to take us back to old Master. I never did have any more good times 'cepting when I'd get to go to visit at old Master's. None of our family could be sold and that was why old Master just loaned us to young Master. When old Master died, dey put all our names in a hat and all the chilluns draw out a name. This was done to 'vide us niggers satisfactory. Young Master drawed my mother's name and they all agreed that I should go with her, so back we went to Miss Jo. She wouldn't feed us niggers. She'd make me set in a corner like a little dog. I got so hungry and howled so loud they had to feed me. When the surrender come, I was eleven years old, and they told us we was free. I ran off and hid in the plum orchard and I said over'n over, "I'se free, I'se free; I ain't never going back to Miss Jo." My mother come out and got me and in a few days my father came and lived with us. He worked for young Master and the crops was divided with him. Miss Jo died and we lived on there. My mother took over the charge of the house and the chillun for young Master and we was all purty happy after that. They was a white man come into our settlement and bought a plantation and some slaves. My, but he treated them bad. He owned a boy about fifteen years old. One day he sent him on a errand. On the way home he got off his mule and set down in the shade of a tree to rest. He fell asleep and the mule went home. When he woke up he was scared to go home and he stayed out in de woods for several days. Finally they caught him and took him home and his master beat him nearly to death. He then dug a hole and put him in it and piled corn shucks all around him. This nearly killed him 'cause his body was cut up so with the whip. One of the niggers slipped off and went to the jining plantation and told about the way the boy was being treated and a bunch of white men came over and made him take the child out and doctor his wounds. This man lived there about ten years and he was so mean to his slaves 'til all the white men round who owned

niggers finally went to him and told him they would just give him so long to sell out and leave. They made him sell his slaves to people there in the community, and he went back north.

My mother told me that he owned a woman who was the mother of several chillun and when her babies would get about a year or two of age he'd sell them and it would break her heart. She never got to keep them. When her fourth baby was born and was about two months old she just studied all the time about how she would have to give it up and one day she said, "I just decided I'm not going to let old Master sell this baby; he just ain't going to do it." She got up and give it something out of a bottle and purty soon it was dead. 'Course didn't nobody tell on her or he'd of beat her nearly to death. There wasn't many folks that was mean to their slaves.

Old Master's boys played with the nigger boys all the time. They'd go swimming, fishing and hunting together. One of his boys name was Robert but everybody called him Bud. They all would catch rabbits and mark them and turn them loose. One day a boy come along with a rabbit he had caught in a trap. Old Master's boy noticed that it had Bud's mark on it and they made him turn it loose.

Old Master was his own overseer, but my daddy was the overlooker. He was purty hard on them too, as they had to work just like they never got tired. The women had to do housework, spinning, sewing and work in the fields too. My mother was a housewoman and she could keep herself looking nice. My, she went around with her hair and clothes all Jenny-Lynned-up all the time until we went to live with Miss Jo. She took all the spirit out of poor mother and me too.

I remember she allus kept our cabin as clean and neat as a pin. When other niggers come to visit her they would say, "My you are Buckry Niggers (meaning we tried to live like white folks)."

I love to think of when we lived with old Master. We had a good time. Our cabin was nice and had a chimbley in it. Mother would cook and serve our breakfast at home every morning and dinner and supper on Sundays. We'd have biscuits every Sunday morning for our breakfast. That was something to look forward to.

We all went to church every Sunday. We would go the white folks church in the morning and to our church in the evening. Bill McWilliams, old Master's oldest boy, didn't take much stock in church. He owned a nigger named Bird, who preached for us. Bill said, "Bird, you can't preach, you can't read, how on earth can you get a text out of the Bible when you can't even read? How'n hell can a man preach that don't know nothing?" Bird told him the Lord had called him to preach and he'd put the things in his mouth that he ought to say. One night Bill went to church and Bird

preached the hair-raisingest sermon you ever heard. Bill told him all right to go and preach, and he gave Bird a horse and set him free to go anywhere he wanted to and preach.

Old Master and old Mistress lived in grand style. Bob was the driver of their carriage. My, but he was always slick and shiny. He'd set up in front with his white shirt and black clothes. He looked like a black martin (bird) with a white breast. The nurse set in the back with the chillun. Old Master and Mistress set together in the front seat.

Old Master and Mistress would come down to the quarters to eat Christmas dinners sometimes and also birthday dinners. It was sho' a big day when they done that. They eat first, and the niggers would sing and dance to entertain them. Old Master would walk 'round through the quarters talking to the ones that was sick or too old to work. He was awful kind. I never knowed him to whip much. Once he whipped a woman for stealing. She and mother had to spin and weave. She couldn't or didn't work as fast as Ma and wouldn't have as much to show for her days work. She'd steal hanks of ma's thread so she couldn't do more work than she did. She'd also steal old Master's tobacco. He caught up with her and whipped her.

I never saw any niggers on the block but I remember once they had a sale in town and I seen them pass our house in gangs, the little ones in wagons and others walking. I've seen slaves who run away from their masters and they'd have to work in the field with a big ball and chain on their leg. They'd hoe out to the end of the chain and then drag it up a piece and hoe on to the end of the row.

Times was awful hard during the War. We actually suffered for some salt. We'd go to the smoke house where meat had been salted down for years, dig a hole in the ground and fill it with water. After it would stand for a while we'd dip the water up carefully and strain it and cook our food in it. We parched corn and meal for coffee. We used syrup for sugar. Some folks parched okra for coffee. When the War was over you'd see men, women and chillun walk out of their cabins with a bundle under their arm. All going by in droves, just going nowhere in particular. My mother and father didn't join them; we stayed on at the plantation. I run off and got married when I was twenty. Ma never did want me to get married. My husband died five years ago. I never had no chillun.

I reckon I'm a mite superstitious. If a man comes to your house first on New Years you will have good luck; if a woman is your first visitor you'll have bad luck. When I was a young woman I knowed I'd be left alone in my old age. I seen it in my sleep. I dreamed I spit every tooth in my head right out in my hand and something tell me I would be a widow. That's a bad thing to dream about, losing your teeth.

Once my sister was at my house. She had a little baby and we was setting on the porch. They was a big pine tree in front of the house, and we seen something that looked like a big bird light in the tree. She begun to cry and say that's a sign my baby is going to die. Sho' nuff it just lived two weeks. Another time a big owl lit in a tree near a house and we heard it holler. The baby died that night. It was already sick, we's setting up with it.

I don't know where they's hants or not but I'se sho heard things I couldn't see.

We allus has made our own medicines. We used herbs and roots. If you'll take poke root and cut it in small pieces and string it and put it 'round a baby's neck it will cut teeth easy. A tea made out of dog fennel or corn shucks will cure chills and malaria. It'll make 'em throw up. We used to take button snake root, black snake root, chips or anvil iron and whiskey and make a tonic to cure consumption. It would cure it too.

Mose Smith

🐝 🐝 🐝

Age 85 Years
Lamar County

I was born in New Orleans, but don't remember anything about that place for I was sold to Master Jack Dunn when a little boy and moved to Paris, Texas. Master Jack and his wife, Suda, owned four pretty big farms around Paris and he was kept busy all the time going around to each of them, with me going along sometimes on a horse beside him. He'd be gone for a week at a time, come home and get some home cooking, clean up and be gone again.

There was twelve slave families on the farm where I lived and the overseers was three. More families on the other places, how many I don't know, but the old master was well fixed with slaves and money, too.

My father was Isom Smith. He lived on a different farm than mother and us children. Her name was Laura and my brother's name was Max; my sister was Rochelle. We lived in a log cabin just like all the other houses on the farm. It was two rooms, one a kitchen, but they both had fireplaces made of mud, grass and sticks, and the biggest piece of furniture was the wooden bed put together with wooden pegs.

Father worked out for extra money and every Saturday night he come over and give each of us children a nickel. That went for the old fashioned kind of horehound candy what we could get in town, or if the sweet tooth wasn't craving for it, we'd get a little can of sardines.

Before I got big enough to work in the fields the mistress would say for me to stay about the big house with her, but Master Jack say, "No, wife, get his sister. Swiger (that was my pet name in them long days), he's going with me." But lots of times they would let me sleep on the floor at the foot of Miss Julie's (Dunn's daughter) bed.

Sometimes I would do pranks around the big house and when the mistress chase me I'd run home and crawl under the bed, telling my mother not to let Mistress Suda get me. Pretty soon the mistress come to the door. "Where is Swiger?" she'd ask my mother. "He's there under the bed!"

Then I'd answer from under the bed: "If you whip me one lick I won't stay with you no more." But I knew all the time she wasn't going to whip, because both the mistress and master was good to all the colored folks. The mistress laughed and say, "Come on out from under the bed and I'll give you a gun." She did, too, a wooden gun that I played with for a long time. She was always giving me things when I was little.

When I growed up a little more they give me so many rows of cotton to hoe or pick. I work my own rows and they timed me so I had to hurry and get the work done, and when they send me off the farm to do a chore they time me on that. Sometimes I would take the axe and split rails for fence-making. There was always something to do around the place.

I even have helped with the spinning and weaving. Mother spin her colored thread and make caps and cotton clothes for us. She sewed the pants by hand and maybe make a coat to go with the pants; that made a pretty nice suit.

One time the master go away on a trip and left me behind. I'd been hearing about slaves running away and it seemed like a mighty good time for me to get away. I just walked off like I was going some place to cut wood. Didn't cut no wood—just kept on going and going and hiding out until I [got] to Louisiana, whereabout I don't know, but long before I got

safe away I was wishing to be back with the master and get full of them good baked sweet potatoes!

And then I got to thinking about how mean Maw was, how hard she'd whip me and I just kept a-going. One time she put a sack over my head, tying it with my arms inside and whipped to the hollow. God, she did whip! She was so mean the master would send her away on other farms for awhile, but she always come back, promising to do good.

That was what I was running away from more than the master. Down there in Louisiana I hid out until after the war was over and then went to work for old Doctor Thomas. Just sort of cleaned up his office and around his home. He was a good man.

I never been married like folks do nowadays. There was an Egyptian woman who had a pretty young girl and she give me the girl to live with. The girl was named Lula and we had three children.

About the war I know nothing, except I heard the folks talking about, but never seen any fighting or battles. We was too far from the ruckus, I reckon.

J. W. Stinnett

☃ ☃ ☃

Age 75 Years
Grayson County

What with raising nine grandchildren whose mammy is dead, this old head of mine has too many troubles to remember much about them slave days, but anyways I was born in 1863, at a place in Grayson County, Texas, name of Prairie Grove.

My mammy come from Virginia, where pappy come from I don't know, and where he went I don't know, because he take off to the north during the war and never come back. His name was George Stinnett and mammy's name was Mary Stinnett. They belonged to a big and fat Creek Indian name of Frank Stinnett who one time lived right around Muskogee here. That was before the War I guess, for mammy told me when the fighting begun the old master bundled up a tent with some food stuffs and moved down to Texas, taking mammy and pappy with him. They was his only slaves and they said he treated them good and fed them good.

That old Indian live in a tent during the summer and cook everything on the open fire, but in the winter he go into his log cabin, coming out once in a while for to hunt squirrels and rabbits for the stew. Mammy said he didn't have much of a farm, just a little patch of garden ground. After they moved to Texas my mammy said she broke the planting ground with oxen, then when pappy run off she had all the work to do in the house and in the field.

Beauregard Tenneyson

Age 87 Years
Gregg County [?]

My mother and father just about stocked Jess Tenneyson's plantation with slaves. That's a fact. The old folks had one big family—twenty-three children was the number. With the old folks that make twenty-five (there were only five more slaves), so I reckon they done mighty well by Master Jess.

The Master done well by them, too. Master Jess and Mistress Lula was Christian peoples. They raised their two sons, Henry and George, the same way.

There was so many of us children I don't remember all the names. Three of the boys was named after good southern gentlemen who soldiered in the War. Price, Lee and Beaugard [*sic*]. Beaugard is me. Proud of that name just like I'm proud of the Master's name.

My folks named Patrick and Harriett. Mother worked round the house and father was the field boss. They was close by the Master all the time.

The plantation was down in Craig [Gregg?] County, Texas. Nine hundred acre it was. They raise everything, but mostly corn and cotton. Big times when come the harvest. Master fix up a cotton gin right on the place. It was an old-fashioned press. Six horses run it with two boys tromping down the cotton with their feets.

In the fall time was the best of all. Come cotton picking time, all the master[s] from miles around send in their best pickers—and how they'd work. Sometimes pick the whole crop in one day! The one who picked the most win a prize. Then come noon and the big feast, and at night come the dancing.

Something like that when the corn was ready. All the folks have the biggest time. Log rollings. Clearing the new ground for planting. Cutting the trees, burning the bresh, making ready for the plow. The best worker wins hisself a prize at these log rollings, too.

Them kind of good times makes me think of Christmas. Didn't have no Christmas tree, but they set up a long pine table in the house and that plank table was covered with presents and none of the Negroes was ever forgot on that day.

Master Jess didn't work his slaves like other white folks done. Wasn't no four o'clock wake-up horns and the field work started at seven o'clock. Quitting time was five o'clock—just about union hours nowadays. The Master believed in plenty of rest for the slaves and they work better that way, too.

One of my brother took care of the Master's horse while on the plantation. When the Master join in with rebels that horse went along. So did brother. Master need them both and my brother mighty pleased when he get to go.

When Master come back from the War and tell us that brother is dead, he said brother was the best boy in all the army.

The Tenneyson slaves wasn't bothered with patrollers, neither the Klan. The Master said we was all good Negroes—nobody going to bother a good Negro.

We was taught to work and have good manners. And to be honest. Just doing them three things will keep anybody out of trouble.

Johnson Thompson

❦ ❦ ❦

Age 84 Years
Rusk County

Just about two weeks before the coming of Christmas Day in 1853, I was born on a plantation somewheres eight miles east of Bellview, Rusk County, Texas. One year later my sister Phyllis was born on the same place and we been together pretty much of the time ever since, and I reckon dere's only one thing that could separate us slave born children.

Mammy and pappy belong to W. P. Thompson, mixed-blood Cherokee Indian, but before that pappy had been owned by three different masters; one was the rich Joe Vann who lived down at Webber Falls and another was Chief Lowery of the Cherokees. I had a brother named Harry who belonged to the Vann family at Tahlequah. Dere was a sister named Patsy; she died at Wagoner, Oklahoma. My mother was born 'way back in the hills of the old Flint District of the Cherokee Nation; just about where Scraper, Okla., is now.

My parents are both dead now—seems like fifty, maybe sixty year ago. Mammy died in Texas, and when we left Rusk County after the Civil War, pappy took us children to the graveyard. We patted her grave and kissed the ground . . . telling her goodbye. Pappy is buried in the church yard on Four Mile Branch.

I don't remember much about my pappy's mother; but I remember she would milk for a man named Columbus Balredge, and she went to prayer meeting every Wednesday night. Sometimes us children would try to follow her, but she'd turn us around pretty quick and chase us back with: "Go on back to the house or the wolves'll get you."

Master Thompson brought us from Texas when I was too little to remember about it, and I don't know how long it was before we was all sold to John Harnage; "Marse John" was his pet name and he liked to be called that-a-way. He took us back to Texas, right down near where I was born at Bellview.

The master's house was a big log building setting east and west, with a porch on the north side of the house. The slave cabins was in a row, and

we lived in one of them. It had no windows, but it had a wood floor that was kept clean with plenty of brushings, and a fireplace where mammy'd cook the turnip greens and peas and corn—I still likes the cornbread with fingerprints baked on it, like in the old days when it was cooked in a skillet over the hot wood ashes. I eat from a big pan set on the floor—there was no chairs—and I slept in a trundle bed that was pushed under the big bed in the daytime.

I spent happy days on the Harnage plantation; going squirrel hunting with the master—he always riding, while I run along and throw rocks in the trees to scare the squirrels so's Marse John could get the aim on them; pick a little cotton and put it in somebody's hamper (basket), and run races with other colored boys to see who would get to saddle the master's horse, while the master would stand laughing by the gate to see which boy won the race.

Our clothes was home-made—cotton in the summer, mostly just a long-tailed shirt and no shoes, and wool goods in the winter. Mammy was the house girl and she weaved the cloth and my Aunt 'Tilda dyed the cloth with wild indigo, leaving her hands blue looking most of the time. Mammy work late in the night, and I hear the loom making noises while I try to sleep in the cabin. Pappy was the shoe-maker and he used wooden pegs of maple to fashion the shoes.

The master had a bell to ring every morning at four o'clock for the folks to turn out. Sometimes the sleep was too deep and somebody would be late, but the master never punish anybody, and I never see anybody whipped and only one slave sold.

Pappy wanted to go back to his mother when the War was over and the slaves was freed. He made a deal with Dave Mounts, a white man, who was moving into the Indian country, to drive for him. A four-mule team was hitched to the wagon, and for five weeks we was on the road from Texas, finally getting to grandmaw Brewers at Fort Gibson. Pappy worked around the farms and fiddled for the Cherokee dances.

Den I went to a subscription school for a little while, but didn't get much learning. Lots of the slave children didn't ever learn to read or write. And we learned something about religion from an old colored preacher named Tom Vann. He would sing for us, and I'd like to hear them old songs again!

The first time I married was to Clara Nevens, and I wore checked wool pants and a blue striped cotton shirt. Dere come six children: Charley, Alec, Laura, Harry, Richard and Jeffy, who was named after Jefferson Davis. The second time I married a cousin, Rela Brewer.

Jefferson Davis was a great man, but I think Roosevelt is greater than Davis or Abraham Lincoln.

Mollie Watson

❦ ❦ ❦

Age 83 Years
Leon County

"Yes Ma'am, Lincoln was a good man. He took us niggers out from under de bull-whup and de patterollers and give us freedom. I think he was de bes' man dat was ever bawn on dis green earth. He was nex' to God I think."

"Well, effen what I'ze heard about Jeff Davis is true he wasn't no good. I don't think he was much punkin."

I remember hearin' a story about how de confederates was about to git whupped and dey was a cullud man dat advised him what to do and jest how he could win de battle. Jeff Davis told dis man dat he was goin' to do jest as he say and do an' effen he win de battle he was goin' to set all the cullud folks free. Well, dey fit de battle and won it. Did he do lak he promised? No siree. He jest wasn't a man of his word.

I sho can remember dem old times befo' de war and endurin' of de war, too. I had a good time as I was jest a little chile and Old Miss sort o' petted me I reckon.

We lived in Centervill[e], Leon County, Texas. My mother was Patience Garner and my father was Wesley Garner. Our owner was Squire Garner and our young Massa was Sebastian Stroud.

Ole Miss was a widow wid three chillen, Sebastian, Linnie, and Betty Stroud, when she married Square Garner. We was all her slaves, ceptin my father and one or two more he had when they married.

Ole Miss and Squire Garner decided to move into town and run de tavern and livery stable. She didn't need very many slaves so she give 'em all out to her children and her brother. She give my mother and my brother and Aunt Harriet's daughter, Dinah, to Miss Linnie. She told my mother dat she'd keep me cause somebody might run over me. I stayed right in de house wid her so long dat I thought ever thing in it belonged to me. I sho' was a spiled youngun.

My main job was to fill and light Ole Miss's pipe and to keep her room tidy. Ole Massa kept my father and several of de men to do de work around de yard and stables and to take keer o' de horses and de kerriges [carriages].

Our house sho' was a nice one. It was a big white house with a long gallery clean across de front of it and it had twenty-four rooms in it. De bedrooms all had a fireplace in 'em and de kitchen set away from de house about twenty feet. Dey was a board walk dat jined it to de house and dis walk was kivered wid a grape arbor.

De furniture was bought in New Orleans. Dey was sofas, lounges and chairs dat was kivered wid red plush wid blue flowers. De carpets was hand woven and kivered de whole flo'.

In de bedrooms was nice furniture, too. Corded beds and chairs and bureaus wid beveled glasses and marble tops, wash-stands wid purty wash-bowls and pitchers to match. They wasn't no springs on de beds. Dey used rope slats and de biggest feather beds you ever seen. Sheets and pillow-cases, pillow shams and coverlids was all hand made.

Dey cooked in pots dat hung on racks in de fireplace. Dey had racks out in de yard where dey cooked sometimes. When dey cooked in dese big pots dey would take a big middlin' o' meat and cut it in about four pieces and dey would boil it wid greens, collards, peas, turnips or beans. Dey cooked corn-bread in a big oven dat was built in de yard.

We allus had a lot o' good things to eat as Ole Miss set a good table for de travelers. I got to eat jest what de white folks et and we had pie or cake or somethin' sweet to eat ever day.

De coffee was made outen rye or corn meal or sweet potatoes that was dried and parched.

When dey made it from sweet potatoes dey would slice 'em and put 'em in de sun to dry lak dey did fruit or corn. When it was plum dry it was put in de oven and parched and den dey would grind it in a little hand mill. It made purty good coffee but Ole Miss and Squire Garner had Lincoln coffee to drink. Dey called it Lincoln coffee because it was real coffee. Dey couldn't afford to serve it on de table as it was too 'spensive.

She had a coffee pot that held four cups o' coffee. Every mornin' I'd git up and make a pot o' coffee then I'd get a tray and put two cups on it. I'd put de cream, sugar bowl and the spoon holder and two napkins. I'd take it to de bed and pour out a cup fer Ole Miss and Squire Garner to drink befo' dey got up. Squire Garner allus drank two cups but de other one was fer me when dey got through with drinkin' their's. Effen dey went away from Home I'd take de Lincoln coffee and de pot and hide 'em. I'd hide 'em under de house on de flo' sills.

Ole Miss's brother married a po' gal and she didn't like it a bit. She say he could a done better'n dat effen he tried. I didn't like her either cause Old Miss didn't. I thought she was po' white trash. Her name was Miss

Jane. I played with all de white chillen and I called 'em all by name. Miss Jane didn't like dat but Old Miss say effen I call dem Miss an' Massa it would make 'em vain.

I sho' loved Marse Bastian's chillen, Billy and Sue. We played together all de time and we got along good. Sometimes we'd git into a fight and we'd all git spanked. Lots o' white folks wouldn't whup dey chillen fer fightin' nigger chillen but Ole Miss an' Marse Bastian sho' would.

Miss Jane told Ole Miss dat she didn't think it was right to whup her chillen when we had a fight an' Ole Miss say, "I done give you folks some niggers and you all de time whuppin' 'em. I kept dis chile fer myself an' I ain't gonna have her run over[,] I can tell you." So effen us chillen got in a scrap we knowed we'd ever one git spanked good an' proper so we allus managed to have a purty good fight befo' we got kotched up wid.

De town we lived in had a town square. Our house was on de south side an' de jail an' de court house was right across de square in front of us.

Speclators uster buy up niggers jest lak dey was animals and dey would travel around over de country an' sell 'em. I've seen 'em come through there in droves lak cattle. De owners would ride in wagons or buggies. Dey would come into town an' camp over night an' nex' mornin' dey would parade 'em round town an' den take 'em to de town square an' put 'em on de block an' sell 'em. I've seen men, wives an' little chillen sold away from each other.

When de sales would be goin' on me an' Billy an' Sue would ride our stick horses up purty close an' watch 'em. I wasn't scared cause I knowed Ole Miss an' Squire Garner was settin' on de gallery a watchin' it jest lak we was an' I knowed she would keep me safe.

Marse Bastian lived on at de farm after Ole Miss moved into town. His house was a big two-story white house. Right behind it was de first quarters where de workin' slaves lived. Next was de quarters where de nigger drivers lived. Nigger drivers was de cullud overseers. Dey sho' was mean. Dey was so biggety an' such smart-alexs an' dey worked de niggers so hard dat all de hands hated 'em. Dey was a lot harder'n de white overseers.

In de lower quarters was de white overseers homes. Dey had very nice boxed houses. Dey was right kind to de niggers but dey give 'em to understand dat dey had so much work to do and dey usually managed to do it.

Once Marse Bastian had a cullud overseer dat was allus beatin' on some one and one day all de hands ganged up on him an' beat him till he died.

De cabins where de slaves lived were not very big an' didn't have much furniture in 'em. Dey had jest one room and dirt flo's. Dey would spread ashes over de flo's an' dampen 'em and pack 'em down so it would be white and smooth.

For bedsteads dey would stick a puncheon in a crack in de wall an' would drive a forked pole in de middle of de flo to rest de other end o' de pole on. Den dey would put another puncheon in de crack o' de wall on de other side an' rest de end in de fork o' de post. Dey would string ropes across dese an' put de beds on dem. Some had cotton beds an' others jest had straw beds. Dey would be one o' dese beds in all four corners o' de room, each bed had only one leg. Dere was a fireplace an' dey used benches fer chairs.

I recollect that my mother's house had one room an' dey was four beds in it. Ma, Aunt Cindy, Margaret, Dinah, an' seven chillen slept in dis room.

Aunt Luce lived by herself an' had more room den de rest and Marse Bastian would let de niggers dance at her house. All de women wore hoop skirts dat come down to de ground. They'd dance an' stir up de dirt an' ashes on de flo' till de dust git in de chillen's eyes an' make 'em cry an' dey'd have to take 'em home an' dis would break up de dance.

We made our own candles. Ole Miss had some tall brass candle sticks. We would polish 'em wid ashes till dey would shine lak gold. She used dese tall ones in de parlor. De ones she used in de bedrooms was short ones.

De black folks used "huzzies." Dat was a saucer like thing wid a lip to it. We'd fill dis wid grease an' take a wick dat was made outen homespun an' plaited. We wet de wick in de grease an' lit it. It made a po' light, too. Old Miss got some little brass kerosene lamps about de beginnin' o' de war.

Didn't none o' de slaves know de A.B.C's. Square Garner bought a man dat had his right fore finger cut off. He say he learned to write an' when his master found it out he had his finger cut off.

We all wore red russet shoes. De leather was tanned at home. Dey'd dig a pit lak a barbecue pit in a swampy place an' take red-oak bark an' beat it till ooze come out. Den they'd take a layer o' bark an' a layer o' leather an' pack in de pit. When de leather became supple it was already tanned. It was den made into shoes. I went barefooted in summer an' winter as I'd ruther do dat dan wear shoes[.]

De women had two work dresses a year an' two changes o' underwear. De white ladies give 'em dey old dresses to dress up in. When de everday clo's nearly wore out dey took 'em an' made baby clo's outen 'em. I guess babies wasn't as tender as dey are now fer dey has to have de finest o' cloth now to make baby clo's outen.

Dey was a big cane-brake close to Marse Bastian's farm an' de niggers uster slip down in dere an have church an' parties. Dey would git happy an' shout an' somebody would hold a pot over dey mouth so de white folks couldn't hear 'em. De Patterollers was afraid to follow 'em into de cane-brake. Effen he did de men would hide an' knock him in de head an drag him out an' say they found him near de cane-brake an' no one would a knowed who done it. De niggers sho' hated dem patterollers cause dey was so mean to 'em. Effen dey caught a nigger off o' his masters plantation dey would beat him lak he had stole a horse.

All de women an' girls could spin an' weave an' nearly all of 'em could sew. We spun blankets durin' de war. We could keep de nappy blankets but had to send de good ones to de army. I was small an' didn't hurt myself at any kind o' work.

Sometimes when Ole Miss was gone Ole Margaret, the cook[,] would give me lumps o' brown sugar to wash an' dry de dishes fer her. She was good to me an' I liked to do things fer her. It would take me all evenin' as dey was so many an' I'd have to climb up in de shelves to put 'em away. Lucy was a kitchen woman, too. She'd try to make me help her an' she'd tell me she'd whup me effen I didn't. I was afraid o' her an' I'd go in de kitchen an' wash de dishes. I wouldn't do 'em good an' I'd always break somethin' so Ole Miss would ask about it an' I could tell her that Luce made me wash de dishes an' I couldn't reach de shelves an' I jest dropped it an' [it] broke. Old Miss git right in after Luce an' she be afraid to make me wash 'em any more fer a long time.

I never knew much about music but I sho' did like to hear Miss Betty play de piano. I never knew what she'd play unless she sung it. I recollect how she played an' sung, "Shoo Fly, Don't You Bother Me," "Granny Will Yo' Dog Bite?" "Dixie," and "Darling Black Mustache." She uster sing good songs too, sech as "Rock Of Ages," "De Lord's A Rock," "Swing Low Sweet Chariot," an' lots o' others.

My father was sold away from us an' his master wouldn't let him come back to see us any more so he married again. He married a woman from de piney woods. My mother never did git married any more.

Ole Squire Garner died durin' de war an' after de war my father come back an' took me to live with some cullud folks close to him. I hated to leave Old Miss an' I couldn't git along with de folks I was livin' with so I run away an' went back to Ole Miss. I had a hard time gettin' back but I made it an' I stayed about six month before he come an' got me again. I run off ever chance I got till finally he took me so far away dat I couldn't come back. I never saw Old Miss any more but I'll see her when I git to Heaven. I never saw my mother any more either.

When I growed up I sho' did like to dance. I'd ruther dance den eat an' I'd go to dances an' dance all night. Father would say, "Git back by day-light an' cook breakfast." I allus did an' den I'd go to de field and chop or pick cotton all day. I could plow or chop wood or do any kind o' work dat a man could do. I don't reckon it hurt me none as I allus felt good.

We'd have log-rollin' an' railsplittins, house-raisin's, corn-shuckin's an' quiltin's. De old women would cook, de young women would burn brush an' de men would roll logs or build de house. After supper we'd dance all night.

The old folks uster scare us wid "Raw Head an' Bloody Bones." I never did see him but it sounded scary enuff to make me want to be good an' quit whatever I was doin.' Lots o' folks carry lucky pieces. It can be a rabbit's foot, a buckeye, coin or even a button. It all depends on how much faith you have in it. For my part I'd ruther trust in de good Lord to keep me safe from harm den in all the lucky pieces in de world. He can take care o' you an' keep yo' safe both here an' in de nex' world whar we will be de same color an' on equal grounds.

Easter Wells

❦ ❦ ❦

Age 83 Years

I was born in Arkansas, in 1854, but we moved to Texas in 1855. I've heard 'em tell about de trip to Texas. De grown folks rode in wagons and carts but de chaps all walked dat was big enuff. De men walked and toted their guns and hunted all de way. Dey had plenty of fresh game to eat.

My mother's name was Nellie Bell. I had one sister, Liza. I never saw my father; in fact, I never heard my mammy say anything about him and I don't guess I ever asked her anything about him for I never thought anything about not having a father. I guess he belonged to another family and when we moved away he was left behind and he didn't try to find us after de War.

My mammy and my sister and me belonged to young Master Jason Bell. We was his onliest slaves and as he wasn't married and lived at home wid his parents[,] we was worked and bossed by his father, Cap'n William Bell and his wife, Miss Mary.

After we moved to Texas, old Master built a big double log house, weather-boarded on de inside and out. It was painted white. Dey was a long gallery clean across de front of de house and a big open hall between de two front rooms. Dey was three rooms on each side of de hall and a wide gallery across de back. De kitchen set back from de house and dey was a board walk leading to it. Vines was planted 'round de gallery and on each side of de walk in de summer time. De house was on a hill and set back from de big road about a quarter of a mile and dey was big oak and pine trees all 'round de yard. We had purty flowers, too.

We had good quarters. Dey was log cabins, but de logs was peeled and square-adzed and put together with white plaster and had shuttered windows and pine floors. Our furniture was home made but it was good and made our cabins comfortable.

Old Master give us our allowance of staple food and it had to run us, too. We could raise our own gardens and in dat way we had purty plenty to eat. Dey took good care of us sick or well and old Mistress was awful good to us.

My mammy was de cook. I remember old Master had some purty

strict rules and one of 'em was iffen you burnt de bread you had to eat it. One day mammy burnt de bread. She was awful busy and forgot it and it burnt purty bad. She knowed dat old Master would be mad and she'd be punished so she got some grub and her bonnet and she lit out. She hid in de woods and cane brakes for two weeks and dey couldn't find her either. One of de women slipped food out to her. Finally she come home and old Master give her a whipping but he didn't hurt her none. He was glad to git her back. She told us dat she could'a slipped off to de North but she didn't want to leave us children. She was afraid young Master would be mad and sell us and we'd a-had a hard time so she come back. I don't know whether she ever burnt de bread any more or not.

Once one of de men got his 'lowance and he decided he'd have de meat all cooked at once so he come to our cabin and got mammy to cook it for him. She cooked it and he took it home. One day he was at work and a dog got in and et de meat all up. He didn't have much food for de rest of de week. He had to make out wid parched corn.

We all kept parched corn all de time and went 'round eating it. It was good to fill you up iffen you was hungry and was nourishing, too.

When de niggers cooked in dere own cabins dey put de food in a sort of tray or trough and everybody et together. Dey didn't have no dishes. We allus ate at de Big House as mammy had to do de cooking for de family.

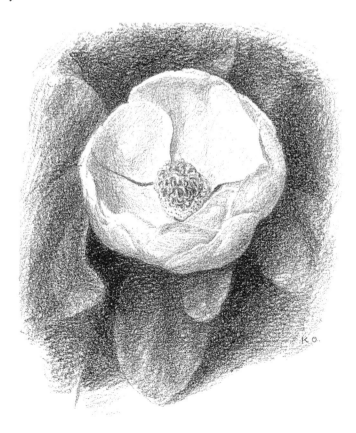

I never had to work hard as old Master wanted us to grow up strong. He'd have mammy boil Jerusalem Oak and make a tea for us to drink to cure us of worms and we'd run races and get exercise so we would be healthy.

Old Mistress and old Master had three children. Dey was two children dead between Master Jason and Miss Jane. Dey was a little girl 'bout my age, named Arline. We played together all de time. We used to set on de steps at night and old Mistress would tell us about de stars. She'd tell us and show us de Big Dipper, Little Dipper, Milky Way, Ellen's Yard, Job's Coffin, and de Seven Sisters. I can show 'em to you and tell you all about 'em yet.

I scared Arline and made her fall and break her leg twice. One time we was on de porch after dark one night and I told her dat I heard something and I made like I could see it and she couldn't so she got scared and run and hung her toe in a crack and fell off de high porch and broke her leg. Another time while de War was going on we was dressed up in long dresses playing grown-ups. We had a playhouse under some big castor-bean bushes. We climbed up on de fence and jest for fun I told her dat I seen some Yankees coming. She started to run and got tangled up in her long dress and fell and broke her leg again. It nigh broke my heart for I loved her and she loved me and she didn't tell on me either time. I used to visit her after she was married and we'd sure have a good visit talking 'bout de things we used to do. We was separated when we was about fifteen and didn't see each other any more till we was both married and had children. I went to visit her at Bryant [Bryan], Brazos County, Texas and I ain't seen her since. I don't know whether she is still living or not.

I 'members hearing a man say dat once he was a nigger trader. He'd buy and trade or sell 'em like they was stock. He become a Christian and never sold any more.

Our young Master went to de War and got wounded and come home and died. Old Master den took full charge of us and when de War ended he kept us because he said we didn't have no folks and he said as our owner was dead we wasn't free. Mother died about a year after de War, and some white folks took my sister but I was afraid to go. Old Master told me iffen I left him he would cut my ears off and I'd starve and I don't know what all he did tell me he'd do. I must a-been a fool but I was afraid to try it.

I had so much work to do and I never did git to go anywhere. I reckon he was afraid to let me go off de place for fear some one would tell me what a fool I was, so I never did git to go anywhere but had to work all de time. I was de only one to work and old Mistress and de girls never had done no work and didn't know much about it. I had a harder time dan when we was slaves.

I got to wanting to see my sister so I made up my mind to run off. One of old Master's motherless nephews lived with him and I got him to go with me one night to the potato bank and I got me a lap full of potatoes to eat so I wouldn't starve like old Master said I would. Dis white boy went nearly to a house where some white folks lived. I went to de house and told 'em I wanted to go to where my sister was and dey let me stay fer a few days and sent me on to my sister.

I saw old Master lots of times after I run away but he wasn't mad at me. I heard him tell de white folks dat I lived wid dat he raised me and I sure wouldn't steal nor tell a lie. I used to steal brown sugar lumps when mammy would be cooking but he didn't know 'bout dat.

On holidays we used to allus have big dinners, 'specially on Christmas, and we allus had egg-nog.

We allus had hog-jowel and peas on New Years Day 'cause iffen you'd have dat on New Years Day you'd have good luck all de year.

Iffen you have money on New Years' Day you will have money all de year.

My husband, Lewis Wells, lived to be one-hundred and seven years old. He died five years ago. He could see witches, spirits and ghosts but I never could. Dere are a few things dat I've noticed and dey never fail.

Dogs howling and scritch owls hollering is allus a warning. My mother was sick and we didn't think she was much sick. A dog howled and howled right outside de house. Old Master say, "Nellie gonna die." Sure nuff she died dat night.

Another time a gentle old mule we had got after de children and run 'em to de house and den he lay down and wallow and wallow. One of our children was dead 'fore a week.

One of our neighbors say his dog been gone 'bout a week. He was walking and met de dog and it lay down and stretch out on de ground and measure a grave wid his body. He made him git up and he went home jest as fast as he could. When he got dere one of his children was dead.

Iffen my left eye quiver I know I'm gwineter cry and iffen both my eyes quiver I know I gwinter laugh till I cry. I don't like for my eyes to quiver.

We has allus made our own medicine. Iffen we hadn't we never could astood de chills and fevers. We made a tea out'n bitter weeds and bathed in it to cure malaria. We also made bread pills and soaked 'em in dis tea and swallowed 'em. After bathing in dis tea we'd go to bed and kiver up and sweat de malaria out.

Horse mint and palm of crystal (Castor-bean) and bullnettle root boiled together will make a cure for swelling. Jest bathe de swollen part in dis hot tea.

Anvil dust and apple vinegar will cure dropsy. One tea cup of anvil dust to a quart of vinegar. Shake up well and bathe in it. It sure will cure de worse kind of a case.

God worked through Abraham Lincoln and he answered de prayers of dem dat was wearing de burden of slavery. We cullud folks all love and honor Abraham Lincoln's memory and don't you think we ought to?

I love to hear good singing. My favorite songs are: "Am I A Soldier Of The Cross," an "How Can I Live In Sin and Doubt My Savior's Love." I belongs to de Baptist church.

John White

❦ ❦ ❦

Age 121 Years
Cass County

Of all my Mammy's children I am the first born and the longest living. The others all gone to join Mammy. She was named Mary White, the same name as her Mistress, the wife of my first master, James White.

About my pappy. I never hear his name and I never see him, not even when I was the least child around the old Master's place 'way back there in Georgia more'n one-hundred twenty years ago!

Mammy try to make it clear to me about my daddy. She married like the most of the slaves in them days.

He was a slave on another plantation. One day he come for to borrow something from Master White. He sees a likely looking gal, and the way it work out that gal was to be my Mammy. After that he got a paper saying it was all right for him to be off his plantation. He come a'courting over to Master Whites. After a while he talks with the Master. Says he wants to marry the gal, Mary. The Master says it's all right if it's all right with Mary and the other white folks. He finds out it is and they makes ready for the wedding.

Mary says a preacher wedding is the best but Master say he can marry them just as good. There wasn't no Bible, just an old Almanac. Master White read something out of that. That's all and they was married. The wedding was over!

Every night he gets a leave paper from his Master and come over to be with his wife, Mary. The next morning he leaves her to work in the fields. Then one night Mammy says he don't come home. The next night is the same, and the next. From then on Mammy don't see him no more—never find out what happen to my pappy.

When I was born Mammy named me John, John White. She tells me I was the blackest "white" boy she ever see! I stays with her till I was eleven year old. The Master wrote down in the book when I was born, April 10, 1816, and I know it's right. Mammy told me so, and Master told me when I was eleven and he sold me to Sarah Davenport.

Mistress Sarah lived in Texas. Master White always selling and trading to folks all over the country. I hates to leave on account of Mammy and the good way Master White fared the slaves—they was good people. Mammy cry but I has to go just the same. The tears are on my face a long time after the leaving. I was hoping all the time to see Mammy again, but that's the last time.

We travels and travels on the stage coach. Once we cross the Big River (Mississippi) on the boat and pick up with the horses on the other side. A new outfit and we rides some more. Seems like we going to wear out all the horses before we gets to the place.

The Davenport plantation was way north of Linden, Texas, up in the Red River country. That's where I stayed for thirty-eight year. There I was drug through the hackles by the meanest master that ever lived. The mistress was the best white woman I ever knew but Master Presley used his whip all the time, reason or no reason, and I got scars to remember by!

I remembers the house. A heavy log house with a gallery clear across the front. The kitchen was back of the house. I work in there and I live in there. It wasn't built so good as the Master's house. The cold winds in the winter go through the cracks between the logs like the walls was somewheres else, and I shivers with the misery all the time.

The cooking get to be my job. The washing too. Washday come around and I fills the tub with clothes. Puts the tub on my head and walks half a mile to the spring where I washes the clothes. Sometimes I run out of soap. Then I make ash soap right by the spring. I learns to be careful about streaks in the clothes. I learns by the bull whip. One day the Master finds a soapy streak in his shirt. Then he finds me.

The Military Road goes by the place and the Master drives me down the road and ties me to a tree. First he tears off the old shirt and then he throws the bull whip to me. When he is tired of beating me more torture is a-coming. The salt water cure. It don't cure nothing but that's what the white folks called it. "Here's at you," the Master say, and slap the salt water into the bleeding cuts. "Here's at you!" The blisters burst every time he slap me with the brine.

Then I was loosened to stagger back into the kitchen. The Mistress couldn't do nothing about it 'cept to lay on the grease thick, with a kind word to help stop the misery.

Ration time was Saturday night. Every slave get enough fat pork, corn meal and such to last out the week. I reckon the Master figure it to the last bite because they was no leavings over. Most likely the shortage catch them!

Sometimes they'd borrow, sometimes I'd slip somethings from out the

kitchen. The single women folks was bad that way. I favors them with something extra from the kitchen. Then they favors me—at night when the overseer thinks everybody asleep in they own places!

I was always back to my kitchen bed long before the overseer give the get-up-knock. I hear the knock, he hear me answer. Then he blew the horn and shout the loud call, ARE YOU UP, and everybody know it was four o'clock and pour out of the cabins ready for the chores.

Sometimes the white folks go around the slave quarters for the night. Not on the Davenport plantation, but some others close around. The slaves talked about it amongst themselves.

After a while they'd be a new baby. Yellow. When the child got old enough for chore work the master would sell him (or her). No difference was it his own flesh and blood—if the price was right!

I traffic with lots of the women, but never marries. Not even when I was free after the War. I sees too many married troubles to mess up with such doings!

Sometimes the master sent me along to the grinding mill. Load in the yellow corn, hitch in the oxen, I was ready to go. I gets me fixed up with a pass and takes to the road.

That was the trip I like best. On the way was a still. Off in the bresh. If the still was lonely I stop, not on the way to but on the way back. Mighty good whiskey, too! Maybe I drinks too much, then I was sorry.

Not that I swipe the whiskey, just sorry because I gets sick! Then I figures a woods camp meeting will steady me up and I goes.

The preacher meet me and want to know how is my feelings. I says I is low with the misery and he say to join up with the Lord.

I never join because he don't talk about the Lord. Just about the Master and Mistress. How the slaves must obey around the plantation—how the white folks know what is good for the slaves. Nothing about obeying the Lord and working for him.

I reckon the old preacher was worrying more about the bull whip than he was the Bible, else he say something about the Lord! But I always obeys the Lord—that's why I is still living!

The slaves would pray for to get out of bondage. Some of them say the Lord told them to run away. Get to the North. Cross the Red River. Over there would be folks to guide them to the Free State (Kansas).

The Lord never tell me to run away. I never tried it, maybe, because mostly they was caught by patrollers and fetched back for a flogging—and I had whippings enough already!

Before the Civil War was the fighting with Mexico. Some of the troops

on they way south passed on the Military Road. Wasn't any fighting around Linden or Jefferson during the time.

They was lots of traveling on the Military Road. Most of the time you could see covered wagons pulled by mules and horses, and sometimes a crawling string of wagons with oxen on the pulling end.

From up in Arkansas come the stage coach along the road. To San Antonio. The drivers bring news the Mexicans just about all killed off and the white folks say Texas was going to join the Union. The country's going to be run different they say, but I never see no difference. Maybe, because I ain't white folks.

Wasn't many Mexicans around the old plantation. Come and go. Lots of Indians. Cherokees and Choctaws. Living in mud huts and cabin shacks. I never see them bother the whites; it was the other way around.

During the Civil War, when the Red River was bank high with muddy water, the Yankees made a target of Jefferson. That was a small town down south of Linden.

Down the river come a flat barge with cannon fastened to the deck. The Yankee soldiers stopped across the river from Jefferson and the shooting started.

When the cannon went to popping the folks went a running—hard to tell who run the fastest, the whites or the blacks! Almost the town was wiped out. Buildings was smashed and big trees cut through with the cannon balls.

And all the time the Yankee drums was a-beating and the soldiers singing:

> *We'll hang Jeff Davis on a sour apple tree,*
> *As we go marching on!*

Before the Civil War everybody had money. The white folks, not the negroes. Sometimes the master take me to the town stores. They was full of money. Cigar boxes on the counter, boxes on the shelf, all filled with money. Not the crinkley paper kind, but hard, jingley gold and silver! Not like these scarce times!

After the War I stay on the plantation 'til a soldier man tells me of the freedom. The master never tell us—negroes working just like before the War.

That's when I leave the first time. Slip off, saying nothing, to Jefferson. There I found some good white folks going to New Orleans. First place we go is Shreveport, by wagon. They took me because I fix up with them to do the cooking.

On the Big River (Mississippi) and boards a river steamboat for New Orleans. Lots of negroes going down there—to work on the canal.

The whole town was built on logs covered with dirt. Trying to raise itself right out of the swamp. Sometimes the water get high and folks run for the hills. When I got there almost was I ready to leave.

I like Texas the best. Back to Jefferson is where I go. Fifteen-twenty mile below Linden. Almost the first person I see was Master Davenport.

He says, "Black rascal, you is coming with me." And I do. He tried to keep his slaves and just laugh when I tell him about the freedom. I worked for food and quarters 'til his meanness come cropping out again.

That wasn't long and he threatened me with the whip and the buck and gag. The buck and gag was maybe worse. I got to feeling that iron stick in my mouth, fastened around my head with chains, pressing hard on my tongue. No drinking, no eating, no talking!

So I slip off again. That night I goes through Linden. Crawling on my hands and knees! Keeping in the dark spots, hiding from the whites, 'til I pass the last house, then my feets hurries me to Jefferson, where I gets a ride to Arkansas.

In Russel[l]ville is where I stop. There I worked around in the yards, cutting the grass, fancying the flower beds, and earned a little money for clothes and eats, with some of it spent for good whiskey.

That was the reason I left Arkansas. Whiskey. The law got after me to tell where was a man's whiskey still. I just leave so's I won't have to tell.

But while I was making a little money in Russel[l]ville, I lose out on some big money, account some white folks beat me to it.

I was out in the hills west of town, walking along the banks of a little creek, when I heard a voice. Queer like. I called out who is that talking and I hears it again.

"Go to the white oak tree and you will find Ninety Thousand Dollars!" That's what I hear. I look around, nobody in sight, but I see the tree. A big white oak tree standing taller than all the rest 'round about.

Under the tree was a grave. An old grave. I scratch around but finds no money and thinks of getting some help.

I done some work for a white man in town and told him about the voice. He promised to go with me, but the next day he took two white mens and dug around the tree. Then he says they was nothing to find.

To this day I know better. I know wherever they's a ghost, money is around someplace! That's what the ghost comes back for.

Somebody dies and leaves buried money. The ghost watches over it 'til it sees somebody it likes. Then ghost shows himself—lets know he's around. Sometimes the ghost tells where is the money buried, like that time at Russel[l]ville.

That ain't the only ghost I've seen or heard. I see one around the yard where I is living now. A woman. Some of these times she'll tell me where the buried money is.

Maybe the ghost woman thinks I is too old to dig. But I been a-digging all these long years. For a bite to eat and a sleep-under cover.

I reckon pretty soon she's going to tell where to dig. When she does, then old Uncle John won't have to dig for the eats no more!

John White

. . . .

127

Acemy Wofford

❦ ❦ ❦

Age Unknown

The folks say I'm about 100 years old but there's no way of me telling about that. I remember the master told me I was born on June 13, but I don't know what was the year. Maybe I know once, but not now, for the only things I remember now is about the master.

I mean my second master who brought me from somewhere in Mississippi to Texas. He was Doctor Hayes; the mistress was Malissa. She was mean, not like the master himself.

When the mistress got mad, and that was likely to happen most any time, the slaves got pretty rough handling. She would pick up anything close and let it fly. Buckets or stone jars, sticks or boards, didn't make no difference, just so's it was loose.

I didn't get around during the slave days. Just worked in the fields like a man and toted water to the master's house. It was a big log house and it seemed like somebody was always wanting water; I wear myself out keeping water in the house.

The night peace was told me I prayed to the Lord. I was thankful. And then after the freed negroes got to leaving their old homes my husband left Mississippi and come to Texas for me. We stayed in Texas on a farm about four miles in the country from Midway.

My first son died during the last year of the war. About three years after the surrender my second son was born and I live with him now. His name is Enlow, same as his father who died December, 1925, in Muskogee.

That's all I know about slave times and when I tries to think more it brings a hurting in my head.

Commentary

L. B. BARNER/LEWIS BONNER

Three distinct narratives exist for the memories of Lewis Bonner, also called L. B. Barner, of Oklahoma City, Oklahoma. The *Oklahoma City, Oklahoma[,] Negro City Directory 1941–1942* identifies him as Lewis Bonner (p. 18). The first two narratives each contain information not in the other; both are presented in this book. The third narrative, not published here, is incomplete but mostly duplicates various facts from the first two narratives.

The first narrative is from an interview made by white interviewer J. S. Thomas on July 15, 1937, which appears in the handwritten manuscript, "Story of Ex Slave L. B. Barner[,] 509 N. Durland[,] Personal Interview," published here, and in the almost identical typescript, "L. B. Barner[,] Age (about) 80[,] Oklahoma City, Okla.," both available in the Slave Narrative Collection in the Archives and Manuscripts Division of the Oklahoma Historical Society, Oklahoma City, Oklahoma, hereafter cited as the OHS Slave Narratives.

The second narrative presented here is available as the text "Lewis Bonner[,] Age 87 Yrs., 507 N. Durland[,] Oklahoma City, Oklahoma." This interview transcript survives as an original typescript in U.S. Works Progress Administration, Federal Writers' Project, Slave Narratives, Oklahoma, XIII, in Box A927, Manuscript Division, Library of Congress, Washington, D.C., hereafter cited as the LC Slave Narratives, and in carbon copy as item 350051 in U.S., Works Progress Administration, Federal Writers' Project, Slave Narratives, Oklahoma, Carbon Copies, Boxes A905–A906, Manuscript Division, Library of Congress, hereafter cited as the LC Slave Narratives Carbon Copies. Another original typescript with the same title and almost identical text is found in the OHS Slave Narratives. The OHS Slave Narratives version of this text bears a handwritten notation, "By Allen," indicating it was undertaken by African American project interviewer Willie Allen. The second Bonner narrative was forwarded to Washington on September 2, 1937, and forms part of the slave narrative collection in the Library of Congress. As with the Bonner narrative, all narratives were forwarded by W.P.A. state administrator Ron Stephens in Oklahoma City to associate editor for the Federal Writers' Project George Cronyn in Washington, D.C., with a dated letter of transmittal. (For this and all narratives in this volume, refer to specific transmittal date, "WPA Note[s] on Interviews[,] Oklahoma Federal Writers' Project—Ex-Slave Narratives" file, Slave Narrative Collection, Archives and Manuscripts Division, Oklahoma Historical Society.)

The third Bonner narrative, not published here, is available in the OHS Slave Narratives. It bears a clipped note which identifies an additional field interviewer, Ida Belle Hunter, an African American staff member with the Oklahoma Slave Narrative Project, who collaborated with Willie Allen on the second interview. The draft, which is a composite of the two narratives published here, includes one sentence which does not appear in either of the other two narratives: "When our grandchillun would visit us, they would call my wife, 'Old White Woman,' and sho made her feel bad."

Lewis Bonner's master most likely was J. M. Swanson, one of two prominent Anderson County planters with the Swanson surname, the other one being H. C. Swanson. A Virginian by birth, J. M. Swanson in 1860 owned real estate worth $4,400 and a personal estate, including thirty-three slaves, valued at $26,500 (Pauline Buck Hohes, *A Centennial History of Anderson County, Texas,* 30–32; U.S. Census of 1860, Texas, Population Schedules, Anderson County, 17, National Archives, Washington, D.C., cited hereafter as Census of 1860, Population Schedules, with individual county names; U.S. Census of 1860, Texas, Slave Schedules, Anderson County, 5, National Archives, Washington, D.C., cited hereafter as Census of 1860, Slave Schedules, with individual county names). For another former slave's remembrance of bondage on one of the Swanson plantations in Anderson County, see U.S. Works Progress Administration, Federal Writers' Project, Slave Narratives, Texas, "Molly Harrell, Ex-Slave," typescript, 1938, W.P.A. Records: Slave Narratives, Boxes 4H359–4H362, Center for American History, University of Texas at Austin, Austin, Texas, this collection hereafter cited as UT Texas Slave Narratives; also available in an abbreviated version in U.S. Works Progress Administration, Federal Writers' Project, Slave Narratives, Texas, XVI, Part 2, 115–16, Box A931, Manuscript Division, Library of Congress, Washington, D.C., hereafter cited as LC Texas Slave Narratives.

The physician mentioned by Lewis Bonner was most likely Dr. H. H. Link, also a slave owner. He had come to Anderson County from Tennessee in 1846 and spent the remainder of his life there (Hohes, *Centennial History,* 34–37; Stephanie Hillegeist Tally-Frost, ed., *Reprint of Biographies from the Lone Star State Published by the Lewis Publishing Company 1893 Containing Biographies of Early Settlers of Navarro, Henderson, Anderson, Limestone, Freestone and Leon Counties, Texas,* 397; Census of 1860, Population Schedules, Anderson County, 33; Census of 1860, Slave Schedules, Anderson County, 13).

Throughout the narratives the interviewees refer to "jean" as the fabric from which slave clothing was made. This material should not be confused with denim used in manufacturing blue-jeans trousers. In the mid-nineteenth century, jean was a woven fabric generally twilled and usually made with cotton warp and wool weft, although it could be made entirely from cotton or entirely from wool (*AF Encyclopedia of Textiles,* 2nd ed., 556; George S. Cole, *A Complete Dictionary of Dry Goods and History of Silk, Cotton, Linen, Wool and Other Fibrous Substances, Including a Full Explanation of the Modern Processes of Spinning, Dyeing and Weaving, with an Appendix Containing a Treatise on Window Trimming, German Words and Phrases, with Their English Pronunciation and Signification, Together with Useful Tables,* 210; Isabel B. Wingate, ed., *Fairchild's Dictionary of Textiles,* 304).

FRANCIS [FRANCES] BRIDGES

Francis [*sic*] Bridges was interviewed in Oklahoma City by an unidentified interviewer from the W.P.A. Oklahoma Slave Narrative Project probably sometime during the summer of 1937. A preliminary draft of her remembrances was prepared as the typescript, "Francis Bridges, Age 73 Years, 314 N.E. 2nd, Oklahoma City, Oklahoma. Home Address: Greenville, Texas," now preserved in the OHS Slave Narratives. The street address given for Bridges's interview was the same as the one for Allen Matthews, possibly her relative. At a later date, also probably in summer, 1937, project personnel lightly edited the preliminary draft to place it into standard form as the text, "Francis Bridges[,] Age 73 Yrs.[,] Oklahoma City, Okla.," published here and available in original typescript in the LC Slave Narratives and in carbon copy as item 350089 in the LC Slave Narratives Carbon Copies and in the OHS Slave Narratives. The final draft of the Bridges narrative was forwarded to Washington on August 16, 1937 (*Polk's Oklahoma City [Oklahoma County, Okla.] Directory 1937,* 920).

Francis Bridges's master was most likely Travis George Wright, who owned fifty-three slaves in 1860 in Red River County. The son of Claiborne Wright, who in 1816 had been one of the earliest Anglo-American settlers on the Red River in present-day Texas, Travis George Wright was known as a prominent planter and promoter of both Red River navigation and local railway construction (William S. Speer, ed., *The Encyclopedia of the New West,* 80–82; Skipper Steely, *Six Months from Tennessee,* 1, 12, 15, 18, 26, 67, 107, 115, 124, 127–29, 145, 151, 156, 162, 164–65; Census of 1860, Slave Schedules, Red River County, 10).

ESTHER EASTER

W.P.A. interviewer L. P. Livingston, a white employee of the agency, interviewed Esther Easter at her home in Tulsa, Oklahoma, on July 14, 1937. Oklahoma Writers' Project staff member Craig Vollmer prepared an edited version of the text of the interview that summer. Vollmer's preliminary draft is available as the typescript "Interview with Mrs. Esther Easter (Slave Born, 1852[,] Age 85) 1438 North Owasso Ave., Tulsa" in the OHS Slave Narratives. From this text project personnel prepared a final draft in standard format. This later version, "Mrs. Esther Easter[,] Age 85 Yrs.[,] Tulsa, Okla.," published here, was forwarded to Washington on September 2, 1937. It is available in original typescript in the LC Slave Narratives and in carbon copies as item 350052 in the LC Slave Narratives Carbon Copies and in the OHS Slave Narratives. Benjamin A. Botkin, director of folklore for the Federal Writers' Project, praised the Esther Easter interview as a "straightforward, well-rounded autobiographical portrait and narrative, giving insight into the life of owners" ([B. A. Botkin], W.P.A. Writers' Project Records Appraisal Sheet Accession no. 530052, December 12, 1940, U.S. Works Progress Administration, Federal Writers' Project, Slave Narratives, Oklahoma, "Appraisal Sheets A-Z" file, Box A905, Manuscript Division, Library of Congress, hereafter cited as LC Slave Narratives Appraisal Sheets; *Polk's Tulsa [Tulsa County, Okla.] City Directory 1935,* 213, 690).

Esther Easter's account of the crack in the wall is one of the most frequently published stories from all W.P.A. ex-slave interviews undertaken in Oklahoma. It appeared in at least four separate anthologies drawn from the national Slave Narrative Project: B. A. Botkin, *Lay My Burden Down: A Folk History of Slavery,* 195; James Mellon, ed., *Bullwhip Days: The Slaves Remember,* 342; George P. Rawick, ed., *The American Slave: A Composite Autobiography,* ser. 1, 12: 89–90; Norman R. Yetman, *Life under the "Peculiar Institution": Selections from the Slave Narrative Collection,* 108. Referring to Esther Easter's trip from Missouri to Texas, the preliminary draft contains a more complete explanation: "The trip was evidently made over the old Military Trail or the 'Texas Road,' as it is commonly called today." For background on this historic route across Oklahoma and into Texas, see Grant Foreman, *Down the Texas Road: Historic Places along Highway 69 through Oklahoma,* 5–46.

ELIZA ELSEY

Mrs. Eliza Elsey was interviewed at Fort Gibson, Oklahoma, by W.P.A. Native American interviewer Ethel Wolfe Garrison in late 1937 or early 1938. The narrative survives in a preliminary draft, as edited by W.P.A. staff member Craig Vollmer on January 5, 1938, under the title "Interview with Eliza Elsey[,] Ex-slave, Age About 77, Fort Gibson, Oklahoma" and in a later version, in standard project format, published here and typed on October 19, 1938, entitled "Eliza Elsey[,] Age 77[,] Fort Gibson, Oklahoma," both of which are preserved as original typescripts in the OHS Slave Narratives. This interview was never forwarded to Washington.

Tom Smith, referred to in the narrative, was Thomas J. Smith, listed as a planter in Grimes County in the 1860 census. This slaveholder, possibly master for Eliza Elsey, was a North Carolina native who owned real estate valued at $24,000 and personal property, including fifty-three slaves, valued at $60,000 (Census of 1860, Population Schedules, Grimes County, 58; Census of 1860, Slave Schedules, Grimes County, 34).

LIZZIE FARMER

Two separate interviews with Lizzie Farmer, born near Mount Enterprise, Texas, are found in the Oklahoma Slave Narratives, and both are published here. The earlier of the two narratives is represented by three distinct typescripts based on an interview with Lizzie Farmer in McAlester, Oklahoma, on October 6, 1936, conducted by white W.P.A. field interviewer Jessie R. Ervin. The three typescripts, preserved as two original copies and one carbon copy, are each titled "Aunt Lizzie Farmer" and have virtually identical content. This earlier interview was never forwarded to Washington and survives only in the OHS Slave Narratives. The later interview, entitled "Lizzie Farmer[,] Age 80 Years[,] McAlester, Okla.," was conducted by an unidentified W.P.A. field interviewer and is preserved as a carbon copy typescript in the LC Slave Narratives and in carbon copy as item 350098 in the LC Slave Narratives Carbon Copies, but it is not found in the OHS Slave Narratives. Although the date of the second interview is uncertain, it was forwarded to Washington on August 12, 1937. The later interview clearly was undertaken with the aid of the Slave Narrative Project list of standardized questions for informants and, with the exception of the story about the hog, which is told in a different version, presents content not included in the earlier interview.

The ring plays and play parties described by Lizzie Farmer, also known as Josey parties, were social gatherings of Baptists or other religious denominations who believed that dancing was evil. At these social functions, singers provided music without instrumental accompaniment for both men and women who moved in circles or rings in a dancelike manner and who often joined in the singing. The energetic entertainment allowed lovers of music to comply with denominational prohibitions against dancing because the play party was considered to be a game and not a dance (Francis Edward Abernethy, *Singin' Texas,* 89–90).

SONNY GREER

Native American W.P.A. field interviewer Ethel Wolfe Garrison interviewed Sonny Greer at his home in Muskogee, Oklahoma, probably in spring or early summer, 1938, for on June 8, 1938, project employee Craig Vollmer edited its text. The only surviving version of this interview is the typescript, edited by Vollmer, entitled "Interview with Sonny Greer[,] Ex-slave, Age 88, 620 North 15th Street, Muskogee, Oklahoma," which is in the OHS Slave Narratives. This interview was not forwarded to Washington project headquarters (*Polk's Muskogee [Oklahoma] City Directory 1932,* 96, 234).

In 1937 Sonny Greer was interviewed by a staff member from another contemporary oral history project, the Indian-Pioneer Project, sponsored by the Oklahoma Historical Society. In this interview Greer related that his parents were named Harry and Loucenda Greer, that his wife's masters had been named Wartham, and that his own master was named Cal Rogers. The correct name for Greer's master is probably Hugh Rogers, as noted in this interview, because the census enumerator in 1860 recorded a planter by this name in Red River County as the owner of ninety-four slaves. A native of Alabama, Hugh Rogers owned real estate estimated at $56,000 and a personal estate valued at $80,000 (Census of 1860, Population Schedules, Red River County, 45; Census of 1860, Slave Schedules, Red River County, 11–12; Soney [*sic*] Greer, interview by James S. Buchanan at Muskogee, Oklahoma, August 18, 1937, Indian-Pioneer Papers, 116 vols., Archives and Manuscripts Division, Oklahoma Historical Society, 63: 236–38, hereafter cited as Indian-Pioneer Papers).

MATTIE HARDMAN

W.P.A. field interviewer J. S. Thomas, a white employee, interviewed Mattie Hardman at her home in Oklahoma City on July 9, 1937. His notes, in typewritten form, were forwarded to Washington on November 2, 1937, with seven other Oklahoma slave narratives. The interview exists as a handwritten text, entitled "Story of an Ex-slave[,] Mattie Hardman[,] 524 N. Bath[,] a Personal Interview," in the OHS Slave Narratives, and in typewritten form, as forwarded to Washington, as "Mattie Hardman[,] Age 78 Yrs.[,] Oklahoma City, Okla." The final edited version, presented here, is preserved in original typescript in the LC Slave Narratives and in carbon copy as item 350029 in the LC Slave Narratives and in the OHS Slave Narratives. At the end of his handwritten notes from the

Mattie Hardman interview, Thomas appended the observation: "She having been taught as a child slave and in after life shows a fair degree of intelligence and almost correct speech." Benjamin A. Botkin appraised the Mattie Hardman interview as "a somewhat distorted view of slavery by one who was born two years before the war" but noted that it presented "a credulous view" ([Botkin], LC Slave Narratives Appraisal Sheets, Accession no. 350029, n.d.; *Polk's Oklahoma City Directory 1937*, 315, 827).

GEORGE W. HARMON

George W. Harmon was interviewed in Oklahoma City by W.P.A. reporter J. S. Thomas on July 3, 1937, and two typewritten drafts of Harmon's narrative are preserved at the Oklahoma Historical Society. A first version is the ribbon typescript, "Ex-slave—Story[,] Reference: Personal Interview of George W. Harmon, 5th & Massachusetts-Oklahoma City, Oklahoma," available in the OHS Slave Narratives. The address given by Thomas as the location for the interview is corroborated by the contemporary city directory, which lists Harmon as residing at 528 Massachusetts Avenue in Oklahoma City (*Polk's Oklahoma City Directory 1937*, 317, 879). The earlier draft was edited and retyped on October 13, 1937 with only cosmetic changes as "George W. Harmon[,] Age 82 Yrs.[,] Oklahoma City, Okla.," and this version is published here. The latter draft is available in original typescript and carbon copy in the OHS Slave Narratives. Oklahoma Federal Writers' Project administrators apparently intended to send a field interviewer back to interview George W. Harmon a second time, as a note bearing the initials of Ida Belle Hunter attached to the initial draft reads, "A re-interview will probably mean more information," while another associated note reads, "George Harmon More Info: 11-5-37." For some reason project personnel seemingly never returned, and George W. Harmon's interview was never sent to Washington.

ANNIE HAWKINS

Jessie R. Ervin, a white W.P.A. staff worker, interviewed Annie Hawkins at Colbert, Oklahoma, probably in spring or summer of 1937, for the Hawkins narrative was sent to Washington from Oklahoma City on August 12 of that same year. The interview is available in two versions, a preliminary one and an edited draft. The typescript, entitled "Interview with Annie Hawkins[,] Ex-Slave, Aged 90, Colbert, Oklahoma," is in the OHS Slave Narratives. The W.P.A. edited draft, forwarded to Washington in 1937 and published here, is entitled "Annie Hawkins[,] Age[,] Colbert, Okla[.]" The edited draft exists both as an original copy in the LC Slave Narratives and as a carbon copy, as item 350094 in the LC Slave Narratives Carbon Copies and in the OHS Slave Narratives. In appraising this interview, Federal Writers' Project Folklore Director Benjamin A. Botkin described the text as "somewhat rambling, fragmentary," although the W.P.A. editor in Oklahoma had rearranged some of the sentences to give the text more coherence (B. A. B[otkin], LC Slave Narratives Appraisal Sheets, Accession no. 350094, 15 December 1940). Despite its organizational problems, Botkin chose an extract from Annie Hawkins's remembrances for inclusion in his 1945 book, *Lay My Burden Down: A Folk History of Slavery* (pp. 164–65, 278).

IDA HENRY

Ida Henry was interviewed in Oklahoma City by white W.P.A. field interviewer J. S. Thomas on July 15, 1937. A preliminary typescript of this interview is available as "Story from Ex-Slaves[,] Reference[,] (A) a Personal Interview, 530 N. Nebraska. (Mrs. Ida Henry.)" in the OHS Slave Narratives. A later edited version of the narrative, differing in transcription of dialect, is in standard project format, is published here. The typescript, entitled "Ida Henry[,] Age 83[,] Oklahoma City, Okla.", is available in original copy in the LC Slave Narratives and in carbon copy as item 350026 in both the LC Slave Narratives Carbon Copies and the OHS Slave Narratives. The Ida Henry interview was forwarded to Washington on November 2, 1937. Benjamin A. Botkin, in appraising the Ida Henry narrative, noted that the style was "colloquial, with one or two false attempts at dialect (e.g., 'me mother,' p. 1)" ([B. A. Botkin], LC Slave Narratives Appraisal Sheets, Accession no. 350026, [ca. 1940].)

The 1860 census listed four individuals in Harrison County named Hall as slaves owners, one of them probably being Ida Henry's master. These people were F. Hall with fourteen slaves, J. B. Hall with five slaves, M[ontraville] J[efferson] Hall with thirty-four slaves, and C. M. Hall with thirteen slaves (Census of 1860, Slave Schedules, Harrison County, 52–53, 57, 59, 65).

LEWIS JENKINS

Lewis Jenkins was interviewed at his home in Oklahoma City by African American W.P.A. worker Ida Belle Hunter on June 15, 1937. A preliminary draft of the narrative based on the interview is available as the typescript "Interview with Lewis Jenkins, Ex-Slave, Aged 93[,] 18 So. Douglass[,] Oklahoma City, Oklahoma" in the OHS Slave Narratives. A note card appended to a later draft of the narrative is dated November 15, 1937. This later version, which incorporates handwritten editorial changes marked on the earlier draft, is available as the typescript "Lewis Jenkins[,] Age 93 Yrs.[,] Oklahoma City, Okla." and is published here. Neither draft of the Lewis Jenkins narrative was ever sent to Washington. A remembrance of Lewis Jenkins from another informant in the Oklahoma Slave Narrative Project is available in "Carrie E. Davis[,] Age 97 Years[,] Oklahoma City, Okla." in the OHS Slave Narratives (*Oklahoma City Negro City Directory*, 94; *Polk's Oklahoma City Directory 1937*, 382, 845).

MARY LINDSAY

Mary Lindsay was interviewed by white W.P.A. worker Robert Vinson Lackey in Tulsa, Oklahoma, probably sometime in the spring or summer of 1937. On August 10, 1937, W.P.A. state administrator Ron Stephens commended Lackey on this interview, along with several others undertaken by personnel from the Tulsa office, as being "among the best we have received." The interview was placed in a final edited form and sent to project headquarters in Washington on August 12, 1937. The preliminary version of the narrative is available as the typescript entitled "Interview with Mary Lindsay, Age 91, Ex-Slave[,] 444 East Newton Place, Tulsa, Okla." in the OHS Slave Narratives. The later draft, only slightly edited, was forwarded to Washington and is published here. It is available in original typescript as "Mary Lindsay[,] Age 91 Yrs.[,] Tulsa, Oklahoma" in the LC Slave Narratives and in carbon copy as item 350092 in the LC Slave Narratives Carbon Copies and in the OHS Slave Narratives (Stephens to Robert V. Lackey, Aug. 10, 1937).

Several other contemporaries of Mary Lindsay also left remembrances of the Love Family and of African American bondage in the Indian Territory. Those sources include Robert Love, interview by Ja[me]s S. Buchanan at Muskogee, Oklahoma, April 13, 1937, Indian-Pioneer Papers, 6: 323; Joe Love, "Joe Love, 705 North 3rd Avenue, Purcell, Oklahoma," [ca. 1937], Indian-Pioneer Papers, 76: 39; Alice Curry, interview by Maurice R. Anderson at Pauls Valley, Oklahoma, December 17, 1937, Indian-Pioneer Papers, 100: 488–89; "Matilda Poe[,] Age 80 Yrs.[,] McAlester, Okla.," available in original typescript in the LC Slave Narratives and in carbon copy as item 350012 in the LC Slave Narratives Carbon Copies and the OHS Slave Narratives.

Census records and other contemporary documents bear out many of Mary Lindsay's remembrances of her girlhood as a slave in the home of William and Mary Merrick. The census of 1860 lists thirty-one-year-old William Merrick of Fannin County, Texas, as the owner of five slaves, ages two, five, seven, ten, and thirty-one, all of them female. This household also included wife M[ary] J. and daughters Lorena A., Mary C., and Nancy A. Merrick. William's real estate was estimated at being worth $3,000, and his personal estate was valued at $1,400. Records show that William Merrick also served as a private in the 14th Brigade of Texas State Troops in the Confederate Army, having enlisted at Ladonia, Texas, on July 6, 1861. As a widow, Mary Merrick returned to Fannin County, Texas, after the war, where in October, 1867, she married E. Jasper Moore, a widower with several children. The blended family then continued to live in the Ladonia, Texas, area. (Census of 1860, Population Schedules, Fannin County, 100; Census of 1860, Slave Schedules, Fannin County, 12; Patricia Armstrong Newhouse, comp. and ed., *Fannin County, Texas, Enlistees in the War between the States, 1861–1864*, 76; Newhouse, *Marriages, Fannin County, Texas, Marriage Book B, Circa 1865–1875*, 30; Frances Terry Ingmire, comp. and ed., *Marriage Records of Fannin County, Texas (1838–1870)*, 21; U.S. Census of 1870, Texas, Population Schedules, Fannin County, 20 of Precinct 3). Tulsa city directories list Mary Lindsay as the widow of Henry Lindsay, residing at 444 Newton Place with her daughter, Mrs. Georgia Freeney, the widow of Wesley E. Freeney. Daughter Georgia worked as a maid for Tulsa clothier Henry V. Holmes (*Polk's Tulsa City Directory[,] 1935*, 239, 295, 353, 621, 685; *Polk's Tulsa [Tulsa County, Okla.] City Directory 1940*, 217, 358).

BERT LUSTER

Bert Luster was interviewed at his home in Oklahoma City by black W.P.A. worker Bertha P. Tipton on June 7, 1937. A preliminary typescript of his remembrances is available as "Interview with Bert Luster[,] Ex-Slave, Aged About 85 Years[,] 512 North Lindsay[,] Oklahoma City, Oklahoma" in the OHS Slave Narratives. The text, published here, was edited in pencil and retyped as "Bert Luster[,] Age 85 Yrs.[,] Oklahoma City, Oklahoma" and forwarded to Washington on August 16, 1937. This later draft is available in original typescript in the

LC Slave Narratives and in carbon copy as item 350082 in the LC Slave Narratives Carbon Copies and in the OHS Slave Narratives (*Oklahoma City Negro City Directory*, 118; *Polk's Oklahoma City Directory 1937*, 438, 874).

Manuscript records document that Bert Luster worked many years for the Oklahoma State Board of Agriculture. He served as janitor for the agency at least as early as July, 1911; he became a shipping clerk by 1918 and retained that position with the board until leaving its employment in June, 1927. Luster's beginning salary was $65 monthly, increasing to $90 monthly in 1919 (Oklahoma, State Board of Agriculture, Annual Report for the Year Ended June 30, 1912, September 25, 1912, typescript, p. 25; Oklahoma State Board of Agriculture, Annual Report for the Year Ended June 30, 1919, August 1, 1919, typescript, p. 3; Oklahoma State Board of Agriculture, Annual Report for the Year Ended June 30, 1920, August 1, 1920, typescript, p. 4; Oklahoma State Board of Agriculture, Annual Report for the Year Ended June 30, 1922, October 15, 1922, typescript, p. 3; Oklahoma State Board of Agriculture, Annual Report for the Year Ended June 30, 1923, May 25, 1924, typescript, p. 3; Oklahoma State Board of Agriculture, Annual Report for the Year Ended June 30, 1924, December 22, 1924, typescript, p. 4; Oklahoma State Board of Agriculture, Annual Report for the Year Ended June 30, 1925, [ca. 1925], typescript, n.p.; Oklahoma State Board of Agriculture, Annual Report for the Year Ended June 30, 1926, [ca. 1926], typescript, n.p.; Oklahoma State Board of Agriculture, Annual Report for the Year Ended June 30, 1927, [ca. 1927], typescript, n.p. All of the above in Oklahoma Department of Agriculture Biennial, Annual, Semiannual, Quarterly, and Financial Reports, Box 1, Oklahoma State Archives, Oklahoma City, Okla.).

ALLEN V. MANNING

Robert Vinson Lackey, one of the white employees of the Oklahoma Slave Narrative Project, interviewed Allen V. Manning in Tulsa probably during the spring or summer of 1937 and forwarded a final draft to Washington, D.C., on August 16 of that year. A preliminary draft of the narrative bearing Lackey's name as interviewer is available in original typescript as "Interview with Allen V. Manning, Ex-Slave, Age 87[,] 1330 N. Kenosha Ave., Tulsa, Okla." in the OHS Slave Narratives. At the top of this typescript an anonymous comment reads, "The Person who edited this must ha[ve been] a dam[n] Yankee." The final draft, slightly revised from the earlier version, was sent to Washington and is published here. It is available as "Allen V. Manning[,] Age 87[,] Tulsa, Okla." in original typescript in the LC Slave Narratives and in carbon copy as item 350086 in the LC Slave Narratives Carbon Copies. After Allen V. Manning's narrative had arrived in Washington, Benjamin Botkin described it as "a philosophical portrait, remarkably understanding and revealing in its insight into slave-master relations" and appraised it as both "thoughtful and powerful" (B. A. B[otkin], LC Slave Narratives Appraisal Sheets, Accession no. 350086, December 12, 1940). He was so impressed that he published virtually the entire narrative in his book, *Lay My Burden Down,* in 1945 (pp. 93–98, 276).

The term "boxed shotguns" used by Manning in this interview refers to board-and-batten–style shotgun houses, a typically African American type of building which employed vertical lumber planks to form the walls of houses one room wide, one story tall, and several rooms deep (John Michael Vlach, "The Shotgun House: An African Architectural Legacy," in *Common Places: Readings in American Vernacular Architecture*, 58–78).

BOB MAYNARD

Bob Maynard was interviewed by an unidentified W.P.A. worker in Weleetka, Oklahoma, probably in summer, 1937; a typescript of his narrative was sent from the Oklahoma City office of the Federal Writers' Project to Washington on September 2, 1937. Only the final draft of Maynard's narrative has survived. It is published here and is available as "Bob Maynard, age 79[,] 23 East Choctaw[,] Weleetka, Oklahoma" in original typescript in the LC Slave Narratives and in carbon copy as item 350067 in the LC Slave Narratives Carbon Copies.

In his interview, Maynard mentions a visit by black abolitionist and statesman Frederick Douglass to Natchez. This may refer to Douglass's travel through the town on his way to New Orleans to attend a national convention of African American citizens held there in April, 1872 (John W. Blassingame and John R. McKivigan, eds., *The Frederick Douglass Papers*, 4: xxiv–xxxii; Frederick Douglass, *Life and Times of Frederick Douglass Written by Himself*, 507–508; William S. McFeely, *Frederick Douglass*, 277–79).

AMANDA OLIVER

Amanda Oliver was interviewed in Oklahoma City by an unidentified W.P.A. worker probably in the spring or summer of 1937, for on August 12 of that year a final draft of her remembrances was sent to the Washington headquarters of the Federal Writers' Project. Only this final draft of her narrative has been located, and it is published here. It is available in typescript as "Amanda Oliver[,] Age 80 Yrs.[,] Oklahoma City, Okla." in original typescript in the LC Slave Narratives and in carbon copy as item 350091 in the LC Slave Narratives Carbon Copies. Oklahoma City directories indicate that Oliver resided at 410 Northeast Fourth with the daughter, Bertha Frasier, mentioned in the interview (*Oklahoma City Negro City Directory*, 119; *Polk's Oklahoma City Directory 1937*, 261, 557, 928).

Amanda Oliver's master was apparently Harrison H. Davis, who was listed in the 1860 census as the owner of seven slaves in Grayson County, rather than another contemporary county resident with a similar name, William Harrison Davis (*Genealogical Biographies of Landowners of Grayson County, Texas [from 1836 through 1869]*, unpaged; Grayson County Frontier Village, Inc., *The History of Grayson County, Texas*, 2: 257–58; Frances Terry Ingmire, comp. and ed., *Marriage Records of Grayson County, Texas, 1846–1877*, 14; Census of 1860, Population Schedules, Grayson County, 108; Census of 1860, Slave Schedules, Grayson County, 10).

NOAH PERRY

An unidentified W.P.A. worker interviewed Noah Perry in Krebs, Oklahoma, probably in 1937. Perry's remembrances were placed in typewritten form as "Noah Perry[,] Age 81[,] Krebs, Oklahoma," but the narrative was never forwarded to Washington. Today it remains as an original typescript in the OHS Slave Narratives; that text is published here. Aunt Patsy Caraway, for whom Noah Perry worked in Texas, was actually Martha J. Caraway (1816–1902), a native of North Carolina who was a widow and operated her farm in Hardin County, Texas, as the head of the household (Mildred S. Wright, *Hardin County, Texas, Cemeteries,* 178; Census of 1860, Population Schedules, Hardin County, 7).

PHYLLIS PETITE

Phyllis Petite was interviewed at Fort Gibson, Oklahoma, probably in either summer or autumn of 1937; the identity of her interviewer is not known. The notes from the interview were placed into typewritten form for which a preliminary draft is available in typescript as "Phyllis Petite[,] Age 83 Yrs.[,] Fort Gibson, Oklahoma," in the OHS Slave Narratives. This draft was further edited into a final draft, bearing the same title, on November 4, 1937; it is published here. It is available as an original typescript in the LC Slave Narratives and in carbon copies as item 350010 in the LC Slave Narratives Carbon Copies and in the OHS Slave Narratives. The Phyllis Petite narrative was sent to Washington on November 18, 1937 and rubber stamped there four days later on November 22 (Stephens to Henry G. Alsberg, Washington, D.C., WPA Notes on Interviews). Another contemporary interview with this informant is available as Phyllis Pettit [*sic*], interview by O. C. Davidson, [probably near Fort Gibson, Oklahoma], February 22, 1937, Indian-Pioneer Papers, 8: 209–12. For an interview with the informant's brother, which has similar content, see the narrative of Johnson Thompson also included in this study.

Phyllis Petite's master was John B. Harnage, who was listed in the 1860 census as the owner of twenty-two slaves in Rusk County, Texas. All of Harnage's children were listed as having been born in the Cherokee Nation (Census of 1860, Population Schedules, Rusk County, 88). A native of Georgia, he owned real estate valued at $6,000 and personal property, including slaves, valued at $15,000 (Census of 1860, Slave Schedules, Rusk County, 25–26).

Phyllis, her husband George Pettit [*sic*], and their children were enrolled as freedmen members of the Cherokee Nation by the Dawes Commission in 1904 (U.S. Department of the Interior, Office of Indian Affairs, Dawes Commission, Cherokee Freedmen Census Cards no. 102, Microcopy M 1186, reel 47, National Archives and Records Service, Fort Worth, Texas; U.S. Department of the Interior, Office of Indian Affairs, Dawes Commission, Cherokee Freedmen Enrollment Application Testimony, file 102, Microcopy M 1303, reel 261, National Archives and Records Service, Fort Worth, Texas).

ALICE RAWLINGS

W.P.A. worker Ethel Wolfe Garrison, a Native American, interviewed Alice Rawlings in Muskogee, Oklahoma, probably sometime in the spring or summer of 1938. Then on June 9, 1938, her coworker, Craig Vollmer, edited and retyped her now lost preliminary material into the narrative, "Interview with Alice Rawlings[,] Ex-Slave, Age 80 Years, 812 So. 7th Street, Muskogee, Oklahoma," published here and available in the OHS Slave Narratives. This interview was never forwarded to Washington.

RED RICHARDSON

Red Richardson was interviewed at his home in Oklahoma City by black W.P.A. worker Bertha P. Tipton on June 11, 1937. From the interview a preliminary draft of Richardson's remembrances was prepared as the typescript "Interview with Red Richardson[,] Ex-Slave Aged 75 Years[,] 917 6th Street[,] Oklahoma City, Oklahoma," available in the OHS Slave Narratives. Later in the summer an edited draft was prepared and forwarded to Washington on August 13, 1937. This final draft, published here, is available as "Red Richardson[,] Age 75 Yrs.[,] Oklahoma City, Oklahoma," as an original typescript in the LC Slave Narratives and in carbon copy as item 350105 in the LC Slave Narratives Carbon Copies and in the OHS Slave Narratives (*Polk's Oklahoma City Directory 1937,* 397, 619).

The name and words to the hymn quoted by Richardson apparently were either garbled by the informant or miscopied by the reporter, for the hymn is titled "Hark! From the Tomb." The actual words of the song are "Ye living men come view the ground where you must shortly lie" (Abernethy, *Singin' Texas,* 112–13; W. M. Cooper, *The Sacred Harp Revised and Improved,* 162).

Towards the end of the preliminary draft of the Red Richardson narrative, the following information about his family was recorded: "I married in 1887 to Julia Lee an' ole tim' sweetheart. We had an' ole fashion weddin.' Lots of good eats. We have five chillun. 2 girl chillun. Luther R. is a barber here in my shop. Johnnie R. is in New York. Newt R. is heah working out at the packing plant." At the close of the earlier draft, field worker Bertha Tipton added the following note: "Remarks: Mr. Red Richardson owns and operates a shoe store with approximately $1,000.00 worth of equipment, and a Barber Shop in the 300 block East 1st Street. When asked how he learned the trade he said that while in Texas he ran a Grocery Store, and learned the shoe trade from an old Dutchman, later he left Texas and moved to Coffeyville, Kansas. While there he worked in a shoe shop, and then moved to Oklahoma in 1891 and settled upon 160 acres of land, later established a shop for himself." *Polk's Oklahoma City Directory 1937* reports that Red C. Richardson and his son, Red Richardson, Jr., operated their shoe repair shop at 311 Northeast 1st in conjunction with barber John Barnwell (pp. 619, 1220).

HARRIETT ROBINSON

Harriett Robinson was interviewed by black reporter Ida Belle Hunter at Oklahoma City, Oklahoma, on June 21, 1937. From her notes Hunter prepared a preliminary draft of Robinson's narrative, available as the typescript "Interview with Harriett Robinson, Ex-Slave, Aged 95[,] 500 Block N. Fonshill[,] Oklahoma City, Oklahoma." It is now preserved in the OHS Slave Narratives. This draft, revised and retyped by mid-August, was among ten slave narratives forwarded from the Oklahoma City office of the Federal Writers' Project to Washington on August 13, 1937. The final draft, published here, is available as "Harriett Robinson[,] Age 95 Yrs.[,] 500 Block N. Fonshill[,] Oklahoma City, Oklahoma" in original typescript in the LC Slave Narratives and in carbon copies as item 350100 in the LC Slave Narratives Carbon Copies and the OHS Slave Narratives. Both the preliminary and final drafts in the OHS collections have a strikeover on the street name, Fonshill, and the name, Lottie, in Ida Belle Hunter's handwriting, replacing it. The 1937 Oklahoma City city directory confirms this correction, for it shows the interviewee residing at 524 Lottie Avenue with Pinkie V. and Homer Gray (pp. 292, 628, 875). After the narrative reached Washington, Benjamin A. Botkin appraised it highly as both "frank and full" ([Botkin], LC Slave Narratives Appraisal Sheets, Accession no. 150100, December 31, 1940), and he selected four extracts from it for inclusion in his 1945 study, *Lay My Burden Down* (pp. 3, 180, 193–94, 229, 271, 279, 280, 282).

Harriett Robinson's mother's master was Samuel W. Simms, who with his wife, Julia, was recorded in the 1860 census as having real estate worth $14,000 and having a personal estate, including nineteen slaves, valued at $14,650. Samuel W. Simms became prominent in local affairs, built and operated steamboats, helped to organize the Bastrop Military Academy, and promoted railway construction. The master for the interviewee's father was Eli C. M. (Meke) Smith, who with his wife, Harriet E. M. Smith, was recorded by the census enumerator in 1860 as having real estate worth $46,500 and a personal estate, including thirty-four slaves, valued at $54,870. Overseer Daniel Ivory was recorded by the census as residing only two dwellings away from planter Smith (Kenneth Kesselus, *History of Bastrop County, Texas, 1846–1865*, 26, 32, 38–40, 48–49, 64–65, 70, 74, 85, 92, 161; Census of 1860, Population Schedules, Bastrop County, 1, 61; Census of 1860, Slave Schedules, Bastrop County, 1, 8). For the remembrances from another former slave on the plantation of Eli C. M. (Meke) Smith, see "Alfred E. Menn[,] Travis County, Texas[,] District No. 9[,] March 5, 1938[, interview with former slave] Nancy Thomas," typescript, UT Texas Slave Narratives.

The rhyme about candidates Giddings and Clark, which Harriett Robinson remembered, was repeated during the disputed congressional election in the third district of Texas in 1871–72 between Democrat DeWitt Clinton Giddings and Republican William T. Clark (Walter Prescott Webb, ed., *Handbook of Texas*, 1: 687).

ANDREW SIMMS

Andrew Simms was interviewed near Sapulpa, Oklahoma, by white W.P.A. worker L. P. Livingston probably sometime in spring or summer 1937. On August 6 project employee Craig Vollmer prepared a revised preliminary draft of the Simms narrative, which is preserved today as "Interview with Andrew Simms[,] Route 1, Box 164, Sapulpa, Okla." in the OHS Slave Narratives. This typescript includes the following information just below its title: "NOTE: This person is an ex-slave, born in Florida, June 26, 1857. Parents: Bill Simms–Kizzie Driver." The preliminary draft itself was edited and retyped into a final version sent to Washington on August 12, 1937. The final draft, published here, is available as "Andrew Simms[,] Age 80[,] Sapulpa, Okla." in original typescript in the LC Slave Narratives and in carbon copy as item 350099 in the LC Slave Narratives Carbon Copies and the OHS Slave Narratives. A note appended to the carbon copy in the OHS collection in the handwriting of project employee Ida Belle Hunter states, "Since this ex-slave was so very young, he hardly knows more to tell."

Andrew Simms's master was William Giles Driver, who as a teenager had come to Texas with his family in 1852. In time he became a prosperous small-scale planter. In 1860 the census enumerator noted that Driver had been born in Georgia and that he had real estate valued at $2,240 and a personal estate, including three slaves, valued at $3,949 ("Company 'F' Muster Rolls," *Freestone Frontiers* [Fairfield, Tex.], 9, no. 3 [Aug., 1991], 33; "Confederate Soldiers of Freestone County, Texas," *Freestone Frontiers* 2, no. 2 [May, 1982]: 8; Lucille M. Driver, *The Driver Families in America, Volume III, Shaw Driver [1754], Giles Driver [1760–70],* 156–57; *History of Freestone County, Texas,* 277; B. B. Paddock, *A History of Central and Western Texas,* 2: 482–83; Census of 1860, Population Schedules, Freestone County, 13; Census of 1860, Slave Schedules, Freestone County, 17).

LIZA SMITH

Native American W.P.A. worker Ethel Wolfe Garrison from the Federal Writers' Project interviewed Liza Smith at her home in Muskogee, Oklahoma, probably sometime during the winter of 1937–38. On January 18, 1938, project employee Craig Vollmer edited and typed her notes into a rough draft entitled "Interview with Liza Smith[,] Slave Born, Age 91, 1705 Pickens Street, Muskogee, Oklahoma," available in the OHS Slave Narratives. Later that year the rough draft was revised and retyped into an intermediate version, "Liza Smith[,] Age 91[,] Muskogee, Oklahoma," available in original typescript and carbon copy in the OHS Slave Narratives. That intermediate draft was further polished on October 19, 1938, into a final draft with the same title, "Liza Smith[,] Age 91[,] Muskogee, Oklahoma." This final draft, published here, was forwarded to Washington and is available in original typescript in the LC Slave Narratives and in carbon copy as item 350078 in the LC Slave Narratives Carbon Copies. About the time of this interview the informant was listed in the Muskogee city directory as Mrs. Eliza Smith, widow of George Smith, residing as 1705 Pickens Avenue in the city (*Polk's Muskogee City Directory 1932,* 176, 259).

LOU SMITH

Lou Smith was interviewed by white W.P.A. worker Jessie R. Ervin at Platter, Oklahoma, probably sometime in spring or summer 1937. From Ervin's notes, a preliminary typescript was prepared entitled "Interview with Lou Smith (Ex-Slave, Aged 83, Platter, Oklahoma)" available in the OHS Slave Narratives. From this version, project employees prepared an edited final draft, "Lou Smith[,] Age 83 Yrs.[,] Platter, Okla.," which was sent to Washington on August 16, 1937. This final draft, published here, is available in original typescript in the LC Slave Narratives and in carbon copy as item 350090 in the LC Slave Narratives Carbon Copies and the OHS Slave Narratives. After the typescript arrived in Washington, Benjamin A. Botkin appraised Lou Smith's narrative as "outstanding for its significance and interest," noting that Smith in her expression had "a sense of the right word" (B. A. B[otkin], LC Slave Narratives Appraisal Sheets, Accession no. 350090, Dec. 5, 1940). He chose three extracts from her remembrances for inclusion in his 1945 study, *Lay My Burden Down* (pp. 39, 50, 154, 274–75, 278).

MOSE SMITH

Mose Smith was interviewed in Muskogee, Oklahoma, by Native American worker Ethel Wolfe Garrison probably sometime in late winter or early spring

1938, for on March 2 of that year project employee Craig Vollmer edited and typed her now lost notes from the interview into the text, "Interview with Mose Smith[,] Slave Born, Age 85, 2202 No. Euclid Ave., Muskogee, Oklahoma," available in the OHS Slave Narratives. At a later date the interview transcript was slightly revised and retyped into final form as "Mose Smith[,] Age 85, Muskogee, Oklahoma," which is published here. The final form is preserved in the OHS Slave Narratives. For reasons not known, this narrative was never forwarded to Washington.

J. W. STINNETT

Native American W.P.A. worker Ethel Wolfe Garrison interviewed J. W. Stinnett in Muskogee, Oklahoma, probably sometime during the winter of 1937–38. On February 3, 1938, her coworker, Craig Vollmer, edited and typed her now nonexistent rough draft of Stinnett's remembrances into an intermediate draft. This narrative, never forwarded to Washington, is published here. It is available only in original typescript as "Interview with J. W. Stinnett[,] Slave Born, Age 75, Route 1, Box 139, Muskogee, Oklahoma" in the OHS Slave Narratives.

J. W. Stinnett's master was J. Frank Stinnett, identified by local historians as an "early settler" in the Pilot Grove community in southeastern Grayson County, Texas. Later the postmaster for Pilot Grove, Frank Stinnett in 1860 was listed in the census as being a merchant with real estate valued at $4,000 and a personal estate, including five slaves, valued at $20,300 (*Genealogical Biographies of Landowners,* unpaged; Grayson County Frontier Village, Inc., *History of Grayson County, Texas,* 1: 75–76, 624; Graham Landrum and Allan Smith, *Grayson County: An Illustrated History of Grayson County, Texas,* 34; Census of 1860, Population Schedules, Grayson County, 46–47; Census of 1860, Slave Schedules, Grayson County, 6).

BEAUREGARD TENNEYSON

L. P. Livingston, a white reporter for the Oklahoma Federal Writers' Project, interviewed Beauregard Tenneyson in West Tulsa probably sometime during the summer of 1937. On August 11 of that year his coworker, Craig Vollmer, edited and typed Livingston's now-lost rough draft into a preliminary draft entitled "Interview with Beaugard [*sic*] Tenneyson[,] West Tulsa, Oklahoma," preserved in the OHS Slave Narratives. Later that summer the text was further polished and retyped into its final form, "Beauregard Tenneyson[,] Age 87 Yrs.[,] West Tulsa, Okla.," published here. The text was forwarded to Washington with nine other narratives on September 14, 1937. Within days of its receipt in Washington, Henry G. Alsberg, director of the Federal Writers' Project, wrote to William Cunningham, director of the Writers' Project in Oklahoma, to commend him on the material and its presentation in the "unusually interesting collection" of interviews (Henry J. Alsberg, Washington, D.C., to William Cunningham, Oklahoma City, Okla., Sept. 21, 1937, WPA Notes on interviews). The original copy of the Tenneyson remembrances in final draft is available in the LC Slave Narratives, and carbon copies are available as item 350060 in the LC Slave Narratives Carbon Copies and the OHS Slave Narratives. In his 1970s compilation of American slave narratives, George P. Rawick erroneously stated that the preliminary version of the Tenneyson narrative in the OHS Slave Narratives was a later draft (Rawick, *The American Slave,* Supplement, Ser. I, 12: lix). The title area on the preliminary draft contains notes from field interviewer L. P. Livingston which were not copied onto the later draft. Above "Beaugard," which appears in the title, is printed in pencil "Beauregard." The following is typewritten below the title: "Note: This ex-slave was born in 1845—Age 87. Correct spelling is probably 'Beauregard.'" Tulsa city directories for 1934 and 1935 provide more details on Tenneyson's residence in West Tulsa, noting that he had no formal street address but lived on the west side of the Frisco Railway tracks south of West Twenty-First Street (*Polk's Tulsa [Tulsa County, Okla.] City Directory 1934,* 475; *Polk's Tulsa City Directory 1935,* 532).

JOHNSON THOMPSON

Johnson Thompson was interviewed near Fort Gibson, Oklahoma, by Native American W.P.A. worker Ethel Wolfe Garrison probably sometime in the winter of 1937–38. On January 3, 1938, project employee Craig Vollmer prepared a revised preliminary typescript based on her notes. It is available as "Interview with Johnson Thompson[,] Ex-Slave, Age 84, Living with Sister, Phyllis Petite, 4 Miles East of Fort Gibson, Oklahoma" in the OHS Slave Narratives. This text was later revised into a final draft, "Johnson Thompson[,] Age 84[,] Fort Gibson, Oklahoma," published here and also available in the OHS Slave Narratives. For the remembrances of Thompson's sister, many of them relating to the subject matter in this interview, see the narrative of Phyllis Petite, also included in this study. For reasons not documented, the Johnson Thompson narrative was never sent to Washington. For another contemporary interview with this informant, see Johnson Thompson, interview by Breland Adams [probably at Fort Gibson, Oklahoma, ca. 1937], Indian-Pioneer Papers, 10: 472–75.

Johnson Thompson's second master in Texas, as already noted in the interview with his sister, Phyllis Petite, was John B. Harnage. In 1860 the census enumerator recorded that Harnage owned real estate worth $6,000 and had a personal estate, including twenty-two slaves, valued at $15,000 (Census of 1860, Population Schedules, Rusk County, 88; Census of 1860, Slave Schedules, Rusk County, 25–26).

MOLLIE WATSON

Jessie R. Ervin, a white employee working in the Oklahoma Slave Narrative Project, interviewed Mollie Watson at Colbert, Oklahoma, probably sometime in autumn, 1937. From her interview notes a preliminary draft of Watson's narrative was prepared as the typescript "Interview with Mollie Watson (Ex-Slave, Aged 83, Colbert, Oklahoma)," available in the OHS Slave Narratives. On November 4, 1937, Ron Stephens, at the Federal Writers' Project office in Oklahoma City, wrote to Ervin to ask if she could reinterview Watson, but there is no evidence that a second interview was ever undertaken (Stephens to Jessie Ervin, McAlester, Oklahoma, Nov. 4, 1937, WPA Notes on Interviews). Approximately a year passed with no further work done on this narrative. Then Ned DeWitt at the Oklahoma City office of the project jotted a note on October 19, 1938, and clipped it to the edited preliminary typescript and sent it to be typed into a final draft. Apparently the final typing was never done. Only the preliminary draft in Oklahoma City is known to survive, and the Mollie Watson narrative was never sent to Washington.

Mollie Watson was a slave in the urban household of Thomas H. Garner and his wife, Sarah, whose son, Sebastian C. Stroud, managed their farming operation in the country. Thomas H. Garner had come to what became Leon County, Texas, as early as 1844. He built the first sawmill in the county and with lumber cut there erected what was reported to be the first house in Centerville, even before the town site was platted. He, Sarah, and their slaves operated a tavern on the courthouse square in Centerville which local historians have called the first hotel in Centerville ("County History from the Lone Star State," *Leon County Historical Collections,* [Centerville, Tex.] 1 [1981]: 3–5, 16; *Leon County Cemetery Records* 2: 54; Leon County Historical Book Survey Committee, comps. and eds., *History of Leon County, Texas,* 10; Lucile Manning and Theresa Manning, "John Patrick Reed Family History," *Leon County Historical Collections* 1 [1981]: 53; Stephenie Hillegeist Tally-Frost, comp., *Cemetery Records of Leon County, Texas,* 9; W. D. Wood, *A Partial Roster of the Officers and Men Raised in Leon County, Texas, for the Service of the Confederate States in the War between the States, with Biographical Sketches of Some of the Officers, and a Brief History of Maj. Gould's Battalion and Other Matters,* 45; Census of 1860, Population Schedules, Leon County, 37, 53; Census of 1860, Slave Schedules, Leon County, 13, 18). For another former slave's remembrances of life in the Centerville tavern household of Thomas H. and Sarah Garner, see the typescript, "Gauther, Sheldon F.[,] Ex-Slave[,] Tarrant Co., Dist. #7[,] 9-16-37[, interview with former slave] Henderson Perkins," UT Texas Slave Narratives, also available in an abbreviated form as "Ex-Slave Stories (Texas)[,] Henderson Perkins," LC Texas Slave Narratives.

EASTER WELLS

Easter Wells was interviewed by white W.P.A. worker Jessie R. Ervin at McAlester, Oklahoma, on September 21, 1937. Ervin prepared a preliminary draft of the interview transcription, available as the typescript "Interview with Easter Wells (Ex-Slave, Aged 83, Colbert, Oklahoma)," available in the OHS Slave Narratives. The text was edited and retyped at Oklahoma City project headquarters on October 14, 1937, as "Easter Wells[,] Age 83[,] Colbert, Okla.," published here. This final draft, forwarded to Washington on November 2, 1937, is available in the original in the LC Slave Narratives and in carbon copies as item 350025 in the LC Slave Narratives Carbon Copies and the OHS Slave Narratives.

JOHN WHITE

John White was interviewed by white W.P.A. field worker L. P. Livingston at Sand Springs, Oklahoma, probably in summer, 1937. On August 9, 1937, project employee Craig Vollmer prepared a preliminary draft of White's remembrances based on Livingston's notes, available as the typescript "Interview with John White[,] 131 Oak St., Sand Springs" in the OHS Slave Narratives. Below the title data, this preliminary draft contains the following information: *"Note:* This ex-slave was born April 10, 1816 (121 years ago), at Augusta, Georgia, on the plantation owned by James White, trader and planter." The day after the preliminary draft was prepared, Ron Stephens, state administrator for the Oklahoma Writers' Project, wrote to the Tulsa office asking that the "best reporter" from the office return to reinterview White "<u>word for word.</u>" In the meantime back in Oklahoma City, a final draft of the White narrative was being prepared by other project personnel who may not have known that a directive had been sent for further interviewing of White. That initial final draft, "John White[,] Age 121 Years[,] Sand Springs, Okla.," was forwarded to Washington August 13, 1937. It is available in original typescript filed with item 350016 in the LC Slave Narratives Carbon Copies and in the OHS Slave Narratives. In Sand Springs, John White was revisited by a project worker, who collected more information with which to expand his narrative. Subsequently a second final draft of White's narrative was prepared (Craig Vollmer, Tulsa, Okla., to Miss Churchill, [Oklahoma City], Aug. 16, 1937, WPA Notes on Interviews), and on November 18, 1937, it was sent to Washington project headquarters. This second final draft, published here, is available as "Revision of Story Sent in 8-13-37. John White[,] Age 112 Years[,] Sand Springs, Okla.," in original typescript in the LC Slave Narratives and in carbon copy as item 350016 in the LC Slave Narratives Carbon Copies.

Evidence indicates that John White was a slave in the household of Sarah and Presley G. Davenport, residents of Cass County, Texas. The census enumerator in 1860 noted that they had real estate worth an estimated $4,000 and a personal estate, including one male slave, valued at $1,600 (Census of 1860, Population Schedules, Cass County, 120; Census of 1860, Slave Schedules, Cass County, 42).

White's account of Civil War fighting has no basis in fact, for there was no battle at Jefferson, Texas. The general index (p. 486) to the 130-volume *The War of Rebellion: A Compilation of the Official Records of the Union and Confederate Armies* notes no fighting there at all, suggesting that the location was confused with another place in which there were hostilities.

ACEMY WOFFORD

Acemy Wofford was interviewed in Muskogee, Oklahoma, by Native American W.P.A. worker Ethel Wolfe Garrison probably in spring, 1938. On May 23, 1938, Garrison's fellow employee, Craig Vollmer, edited her notes into a preliminary typescript entitled "Interview with Acemy Wofford[,] 1713 Tamaroy St., Muskogee, Oklahoma," published here and available in the OHS Slave Narratives. The Wofford interview remained in this stage of preparation and was never forwarded to Washington. Garrison apparently misinterpreted the name of the street on which Mrs. Wofford lived, for she resided at 1713 Tamaroa Street in Muskogee in the home of Joseph, Henry S., and Anna Wofford (*Polk's Muskogee City Directory 1932*, 202, 267).

Bibliography

Abernethy, Francis Edward. *Singin' Texas*. Dallas: E-Heart Press, 1983.

AF Encyclopedia of Textiles. 2nd ed. Englewood Cliffs, N.J.: Prentice-Hall, Inc., 1972.

Bailey, David Thomas. "A Divided Prism: Two Sources of Black Testimony on Slavery." *Journal of Southern History* 46, no. 3 (August, 1980): 381–404.

Baker, T. Lindsay, and Julie P. Baker, eds. *The W. P. A. Oklahoma Slave Narratives*. Norman: University of Oklahoma Press, 1996.

Barr, Alwyn. *Black Texans: A History of Negroes in Texas, 1528–1971*. Austin: Jenkins Publishing Co., 1973.

Blassingame, John W. "Using the Testimony of Ex-Slaves: Approaches and Problems." *Journal of Southern History* 41, no. 4 (November, 1975): 473–92.

———, and John R. McKivigan, eds. *The Frederick Douglass Papers*. 5 vols. New Haven: Yale University Press, 1979–92.

Botkin, B. A. *Lay My Burden Down: A Folk History of Slavery.* Chicago: University of Chicago Press, 1945.

———. "The Slave as His Own Interpreter." *Library of Congress Quarterly Review of Current Acquisitions* 2, no. 1 (July/September, 1944): 37–63.

Campbell, Randolph B. *An Empire for Slavery: The Peculiar Institution in Texas, 1821–1865*. Baton Rouge: Louisiana State University Press, 1989.

Cole, George S. *A Complete Dictionary of Dry Goods and History of Silk, Cotton, Linen, Wool and Other Fibrous Substances, Including a Full Explanation of the Modern Processes of Spinning, Dyeing and Weaving, with an Appendix Containing a Treatise on Window Trimming, German Words and Phrases, with Their English Pronunciation and Signification, Together with Useful Tables*. Rev. ed. Chicago: W. B. Conkey Company, 1892.

"Company 'F' Muster Rolls." *Freestone Frontiers* (Fairfield, Tex.) 11, no. 3 (August, 1991): 32–36.

"Confederate Soldiers of Freestone County, Texas." Parts 1 and 2. *Freestone Frontiers* 2, no. 2 (May, 1982): 7–8; no. 3 (August, 1982): 14–15.

Cooper, W. M. *The Sacred Harp Revised and Improved.* Dothan, Ala.: W. M. Cooper and Company, 1909.

"County History from the Lone Star State." *Leon County Historical Collections* (Centerville, Tex.) 1 (1981): 1–39.

Douglass, Frederick. *Life and Times of Frederick Douglass Written by Himself.* New rev. ed. Boston: DeWolfe, Fiske, and Company, 1892.

Driver, Lucille M. *The Driver Families in America, Volume III, Shaw Driver (1754), Giles Driver (1760–70).* n.p.: privately printed, 1992.

Escott, Paul D. "The Arts and Science of Reading WPA Slave Narratives." In *The Slave's Narrative,* edited by Charles T. Davis and Henry Louis Gates, Jr. New York: Oxford University Press, 1985.

———. *Slavery Remembered: A Record of Twentieth-Century Slave Narratives.* Chapel Hill: University of North Carolina Press, 1979.

Foreman, Grant. *Down the Texas Road: Historic Places along Highway 69 through Oklahoma.* Historic Oklahoma Series no. 2. Norman: University of Oklahoma Press, 1936.

Genealogical Biographies of Landowners of Grayson County, Texas (from 1836 through 1869). Sherman, Tex.: Oak Room Emporium Press, 1967.

Grayson County Frontier Village, Inc. *The History of Grayson County, Texas.* 2 vols. [Sherman, Tex.]: Grayson County Frontier Village, Inc., 1979–81.

History of Freestone County, Texas. [Fairfield, Tex.]: Freestone County Historical Commission, 1978.

Hohes, Pauline Buck. *A Centennial History of Anderson County, Texas.* San Antonio: Naylor Company, 1936.

Indian-Pioneer Papers. Typescripts. 116 vols. Archives and Manuscripts Division, Oklahoma Historical Society, Oklahoma City, Okla.

Ingmire, Frances Terry, comp. and ed. *Marriage Records of Fannin County, Texas (1838–1870).* St. Louis: privately printed, 1978.

———. *Marriage Records of Grayson County, Texas, 1846–1877.* St. Louis: privately printed, 1974.

Kesselus, Kenneth. *History of Bastrop County, Texas, 1846–1865.* Austin: Jenkins Publishing Company, 1987.

Landrum, Graham, and Allan Smith. *Grayson County: An Illustrated History of Grayson County, Texas.* 2nd ed. Fort Worth: Historical Publishers, 1967.

Leon County Cemetery Records. 2 vols. Centerville, Tex.: Leon County Genealogical Society, 1982.

Leon County Historical Book Survey Committee, comp. and ed. *History of Leon County, Texas.* Dallas: Curtis Media Corporation, 1986.

McFeely, William S. *Frederick Douglass.* New York: W. W. Norton and Company, 1991.

Mangione, Jerre. *The Dream and the Deal: The Federal Writers' Project, 1935–1943.* Boston: Little, Brown and Company, 1972.

Manning, Lucile, and Theresa Manning. "John Patrick Reed Family History." *Leon County Historical Collections* 1 (1981): 53.

Mellon, James, ed. *Bullwhip Days: The Slaves Remember.* New York: Weidenfeld and Nicholson, 1988.

Newhouse, Patricia Armstrong, comp. and ed. *Fannin County, Texas, Enlistees in the War between the States, 1861–1864.* Honey Grove, Tex.: Newhouse Publications, 1984.

———. *Marriages, Fannin County, Texas, Marriage Book B, Circa 1865–1875.* Honey Grove, Tex.: Newhouse Publications Company, 1983.

Oklahoma City, Oklahoma[,] Negro City Directory 1941–1942. Oklahoma City: Oklahoma City Negro Chamber of Commerce, 1941.

Oklahoma State Board of Agriculture. Annual Reports for the Years Ended June 30, 1912, 1919–20, 1922–27. Typescripts and manuscripts. Oklahoma Department of Agriculture Biennial, Annual, Semiannual, Quarterly, and Financial Reports, Box 1. Oklahoma State Archives, Oklahoma City.

Paddock, B. B. *A History of Central and Western Texas.* 2 vols. Chicago: Lewis Publishing Company, 1911.

Penkower, Monty Noam. *The Federal Writers' Project: A Study in Government Patronage of the Arts.* Urbana: University of Illinois Press, 1977.

Polk's Muskogee (Oklahoma) City Directory 1932. Kansas City: R. L. Polk and Company, 1932.

Polk's Oklahoma City (Oklahoma County, Okla.) Directory 1937. Kansas City: R. L. Polk and Company, 1937.

Polk's Tulsa (Tulsa County, Okla.) City Directory 1934. Kansas City: R. L. Polk and Company, 1934.

Polk's Tulsa (Tulsa County, Okla.) City Directory 1935. Kansas City: R. L. Polk and Company, 1935.

Polk's Tulsa (Tulsa County, Okla.) City Directory 1940. Kansas City: R. L. Polk and Company, 1940.

Rawick, George P., ed. *The American Slave: A Composite Autobiography.* 41 vols. Westport, Conn.: Greenwood Press, 1972–79.

Silverthorne, Elizabeth. *Plantation Life in Texas.* College Station: Texas A&M University Press, 1986.

Slave Narrative Collection. See U.S. Works Progress Administration, Federal Writers' Project, Slave Narratives.

Soapes, Thomas F. "The Federal Writers' Project Slave Interviews: Useful Data of Misleading Source." Oral History Review (1977): 33–38.

Speer, William S., ed. *The Encyclopedia of the New West.* Marshall, Tex.: United States Biographical Publishing Company, 1881.

Steely, Skipper. *Six Months from Tennessee.* Paris, Tex.: Claiborne Wright Historical Association, 1982.

Tally-Frost, Stephanie Hillegeist, comp. *Cemetery Records of Leon County, Texas.* n.p.: privately printed, 1967.

———, ed. *Reprint of Biographies from the Lone Star State Published by the Lewis Publishing Company 1893 Containing Biographies of Early Settlers of Navarro, Henderson, Anderson, Limestone, Freestone and Leon Counties, Texas.* n.p.: privately printed, 1966.

Tyler, Ronnie C., and Lawrence R. Murphy, eds. *The Slave Narratives of Texas.* Austin: Encino Press, 1974.

U.S. Census of 1860. Texas. Population Schedules. National Archives, Washington, D.C.

———. Census of 1860. Texas. Slave Schedules. National Archives, Washington, D.C.

———. Census of 1870. Texas. Population Schedules. National Archives, Washington, D.C.

———. Department of the Interior. Office of Indian Affairs. Dawes Commission. Cherokee Freedmen Census Cards. National Archives, Fort Worth, Tex.

———. Department of the Interior. Office of Indian Affairs. Dawes Commission. Cherokee Freedmen Enrollment Testimony. National Archives. Fort Worth, Texas.

———. Department of War. *The War of Rebellion: A Compilation of the Official Records of the Union and Confederate Armies.* 130 vols. Washington, D.C.: Government Printing Office, 1880–1901.

———. Works Progress Administration. Federal Writers' Project. Slave Narratives. Oklahoma. "Appraisal Sheets A–Y" File. Box A905. Manuscript Division, Library of Congress, Washington, D.C.

———. Works Progress Administration. Federal Writers' Project. Slave Narratives. Oklahoma. Carbon Copies. Boxes A905–A906. Manuscript Division, Library of Congress, Washington, D.C.

———. Works Progress Administration. Federal Writers' Project. Slave Narratives. Oklahoma. Slave Narrative Collection, Archives and Manuscripts Division, Oklahoma Historical Society, Oklahoma City.

———. Works Progress Administration. Federal Writers' Project. Slave Narratives. Oklahoma, XIII. Box A927. Manuscript Division, Library of Congress, Washington, D.C.

———. Works Progress Administration. Federal Writers' Project. Slave Narratives. Texas. W. P. A. Records, Slave Narratives. Boxes 4H259–4H362. Center for American History, University of Texas at Austin, Austin, Tex.

———. Works Progress Administration. Federal Writers' Project. Slave Narratives, Texas, XVI. Boxes A930–A932. Manuscript Division, Library of Congress, Washington, D.C.

Vlach, John Michael. "The Shotgun House: An African Architectural Legacy." In *Common Places: Readings in American Vernacular Architecture,* 58–78, edited by Dell Upton and John Michael Vlach. Athens: University of Georgia Press, 1986.

Webb, Walter Prescott, ed. *The Handbook of Texas.* 2 vols. Austin: Texas State Historical Association, 1952.

Wingate, Isabel B., ed. *Fairchild's Dictionary of Textiles.* New York: Fairchild Publications, Inc., 1967.

Wood, W. D. *A Partial Roster of the Officers and Men Raised in Leon County, Texas, for the Service of the Confederate States in the War between the States, with Biographical Sketches of Some of the Officers, and a Brief History of Maj. Gould's Battalion and Other Matters.* n.p.: 1899.

Woodward, C. Vann. "History from Slave Sources." *American Historical Review* 79, no. 2 (April, 1974): 470–81.

Wright, Mildred S. *Hardin County, Texas, Cemeteries.* Beaumont: Southeast Texas Genealogical and Historical Society, 1976.

Yetman, Norman R. "The Background of the Slave Narrative Collection." *American Quarterly* 19, no. 3 (Fall, 1967): 534–53.

———. *Voices from Slavery: Selections from the Slave Narratives Collection of the Library of Congress.* New York: Holt, Rinehart, and Winston, Inc., 1970. Paperback edition available as *Life under the "Peculiar Institution": Selections from the Slave Narrative Collection.* New York: Holt, Rinehart, and Winston, Inc., 1970.

INDEX

Creek Nation, 49, 58
Cronyn, George, 129
Cunningham, William, 143
curses, 18

Dallas, Tex., domestic service in, 13
dancing, 18–19, 113; at Christmas celebrations, 87; at corn shuckings, 36, 64, 114; at cotton pickings, 9, 103; at Josey parties, 22; at log rollings, 103, 114; music from fiddlers for, 107; and prohibition by some religious denominations, 132; in slave quarters, 112; at weddings, 23, 77
Davenport, Presley, XXVI, 121, 123, 126, 146
Davenport, Sarah, 120–21, 146
Davis, Carrie E., 135
Davis, Harrison H., 64, 138
Davis, Jefferson: ambivalent attitudes toward, 9, 24, 37, 42, 52, 87; child named after, 107; negative attitudes toward, 62, 82, 108; positive attitude toward, 107; song about, 65, 125; story about, 108
Davis, William Harrison, 138
Dawes Commission, 49, 139
Decker (slaveholder in Bastrop County, Tex.), 85
Deckers, Jane, 42
Dewan (uncle of Lewis Jenkins), 39
DeWitt, Ned, 144
Dick, Uncle (slave of Harrison Davis), 64
diet. See foodways
dogs, 40; and eating slaves' food, 116; howling by, as sign of pending death, 118; as slave hounds, 4, 50, 55–56, 76, 85
Douglass, Frederick, 138; negative attitude toward, 87; speech by, 62
Driver, Frank, 88–89
Driver, George, 88–89
Driver, Julia, 88–89
Driver, Kizzie, 141
Driver, Mary, 88–89
Driver, William Giles, 88–89, 141–42
drivers. See overseers, drivers, and foremen
Dunn, Jack, 99–100
Dunn, Julie, 99
Dunn, Suda, 99–100

Easter, Esther, 10–13, 131–32
education: after emancipation, 51–52, 69, 81, 107; and masters prohibiting, 26, 39–40, 42, 81, 85, 89, 112

Elmore, Jim, 50
Elmore, Mariah, 50
Elms Court (plantation in Cass County, Tex.), 79
Elsey, Eliza, XII, XXIV, XXV, XXVII, 14–16, 132
Elsey, Robert, 16
emancipation, 37; and delay by masters, XXX, 77, 79, 82, 117–18, 125; remembrances of, XXX, 4, 5, 12–13, 16, 26, 28, 32, 41, 48, 58, 62, 64, 76, 86, 91, 93, 128. See also freedom
Emancipation Day. See holidays: Juneteenth as
English, George A., 17
English, Harriet, 17
entertainment. See dancing; fishing; hunting; holidays; music and songs; recreation; work amusements
Ervin, Jessie R., XI–XII, 132, 134, 142, 144, 145
Eufala, Okla., 17

Fairfield, Tex., 88
Falls County, Tex., remembrances of, 60–63
families: and reuniting after separation, 48–49, 128; and separation by slavery, XXVI–XXVII, 38–39, 43–49, 66–67, 69, 73, 76, 81, 92, 93, 108, 111, 113, 115, 120–21, 123; as sources of strength for members, XXVI
Fannin County, Tex., 136; remembrances of, 10–13, 43–49
Farmer, Lizzie, XIV, XXIV, 17–24, 132–33
Federal Writers' Project, IX, X, 129–30; editorial process of, XI–XII, XIII; interview transcripts from, X; personnel composition of, IX, XI–XII; quality of Oklahoma narratives in, XII; questionnaires used in, X–XI; and Slave Narrative Project, IX–XV
fences, 117
ferries, 38–39, 12
fishing, 95
Florida, 141; remembrances of, 88
foodways: of American Indians, 102; of blacks, XXIII–XXIV, 3–4, 5, 7, 15, 18, 21, 22, 31, 40, 50–51, 57, 61, 64, 74, 81, 83, 88, 90, 95, 97, 99, 100–101, 107, 109, 113, 115–16, 118, 121, 123; at Christmas, 118; and

Hall, John, 34–37
Hall, Lea, 35
Hall, Lottie, 34
Hall, Loyo, 34
Hall, Margrette, 34
Hall, M[ontraville] J[efferson], 135
Hall, Silas, 34
Hand, Trot, 55
Hardin County, Tex., 139; remembrances of, 70–71
Hardman, Mattie, 27–28, 133–34
Harmon, George W., xxi, 29–30, 134
Harnage, Bell, 76
Harnage, Ida, 76
Harnage, John B., 73–74, 76–77, 105, 107, 139, 144
Harnage, Maley, 76
Harnage, Mary, 76
Harnage, Will, 76
Harrell, Molly, 130
Harrison County, Tex., 135; remembrances of, 34–37
hats. See clothing
Hawkins, Annie, xxiv, xxv, xxviii–xxix, 31–33, 134
Hayes, Doctor (slaveholder in Texas), 128
Hayes, Malissa, 128
Headsmith, Mister (lover of Esther Easter's mistress), 12
health care. See medical practices
Henderson, Millie, 34
Henry, Eliza, 80
Henry, Ida, xxv, xxvii, xxviii, xxix, 34–37, 135
hogs, 71, 82; killed by slaves, 15–16; stolen by slaves, 17–18, 24, 36; stolen by whites, 36
holidays: birthdays as, 97; Christmas as, xxii, 4, 25, 51, 76, 82, 87, 97, 103–104, 118; Juneteenth as, xxx, 41; New Year as, 4, 118; weekends as, 82
Holmes, Henry V., 136
Honey Grove, Tex., 44
horses, 60, 74, 79, 97, 104, 107; injury from, 47
house servants. See work skills
Houston, Tex., 86
Howard, Dock, 34
Howard, Mildred, 27–28
Howard, William Henry, 27–28
Hulbert, Okla., 73

Humphries, Ann, 90
Humphries, Ben, 90
Humphries, Charley, 90
Humphries, Mealey, 90
Hunter, Ida Belle, xi, 130, 134, 135, 140, 141
hunting, 40, 74, 95, 102, 107

Indian-Pioneer Papers (Oklahoma Historical Society), 133, 136, 139, 144
Indian Territory. See Oklahoma
Indians. See American Indians
insanity, 38
Isom, Uncle (slave in Bastrop County, Tex.), xxix, 85–86
Ivory, Daniel, 86, 141

Jackson, Major (slaveholder at Linden, Tex.), xxiii, 78, 79, 80
Jackson, Winnie, 7
Jane, Miss (daughter-in-law of Sarah Garner), 111
jean (fabric), 31, 130
Jefferson, Tex.: garbled account of Civil War fighting at, 125, 146
Jenkins, Delia, 52
Jenkins, Jane, 38
Jenkins, Joe, 38
Jenkins, Lewis, 38–42, 135
Jenkins, Lije, 38
Jenkins, Tom, 38
John (slave at Mount Enterprise, Tex.), 17–18, 24
John, Unkle [sic] (slave in Anderson County, Tex.), 3
Josey parties, 22, 132
Juneteenth (Emancipation Day), xxx, 41

kidnapping of slaves, 89
Klu Klux Klan, 8, 22, 42, 51–52, 61–62, 69, 86
Krebs, Okla., as location for interviews, 138; remembrances of, 71–72

labor practices: and sharecropping, 5, 16, 58; and tenancy, 9; and work for money, 25, 26, 48, 65, 70, 78, 83, 86, 99; and work for room and board, 48, 70
Lackey, Robert Vinson, xi
Ladonia, Tex., 7, 136
Lafayette, La., remembrances of, 56–57
Lamar County, Tex., remembrances of, 99–101